The
Select Letters
of
Major Jack Downing

by
Seba Smith

LITERATURE HOUSE / GREGG PRESS
Upper Saddle River, N. J.

Republished in 1970 by
LITERATURE HOUSE
an imprint of The Gregg Press
121 Pleasant Avenue
Upper Saddle River, N. J. 07458

Standard Book Number—8398-1868-8
Library of Congress Card—77-104567

Printed in United States of America

SEBA SMITH

Seba Smith, creator of the Yankee type in American humor, was born in the village of Buckfield, Maine, in 1792, the son of an impoverished post-rider. When he was seven, the family moved to Bridgton, where Seba worked his way through school. From the age of eighteen to twenty-three he taught school and worked at various trades. Thanks to the generosity of a gentleman from Portland, he was able to attend Bowdoin College and graduated with honors in 1818. He then returned to teaching for a year, and also wrote some poems which were published by the *Eastern Argus* of Portland, Maine. The next few years were spent traveling in the Midwest, New England, and England. An editorial position on the *Eastern Argus* followed. In 1823 he married Elizabeth Oakes Prince, who was to make a name for herself as a novelist, poet, and suffragette. Three years later he sold his interest in the *Argus* and attempted to earn his living by writing. In 1829 he set himself up as a newspaper publisher by founding the *Family Reader* and the *Portland Courier*. It was in the latter that his "Major Jack Downing letters" began to appear: "a national event," according to Fred Pattee. The first letters were gentle satires on the people whom he knew intimately: the small-town and rural Yankees of Maine. These were succeeded by satires on the Washington scene during the turbulent years of Jackson's administration. The "bank war" between the advocates of the Hamiltonian system and the supporters of decentralization receives some wry comments from the "Major," as does Jackson's "kitchen cabinet." The letters were a tremendous success and were reprinted in papers throughout the country. Imitations soon appeared. Charles Augustus Davis, a New York businessman and journalist, and an enemy of Jackson, wrote a series of "Major Downing" letters for the *Daily Advertiser*, and it was not long before the public was thoroughly confused by the proliferation of "Major Downings." Wright's *American Fiction* lists the following books by Smith: *John Smith's Letters, with "Picters" to Match...* (1839), *Letters Written During the President's Tour "Down East," by Myself, Major Jack Downing...*(1833), *The Life and Writings of Major Jack Downing of Downingville, Away Down East in the State of Maine...*(1833), *May-Day in New York...*(1845), *The Select Letters of Major Jack Downing* (1834), *My Thirty Years Out of the Senate* (1859), and *'Way Down East* (1854).

Smith lost his investment in the *Courier* in the financial panic of 1837, and tried to recoup his fortunes by selling a cotton-cleaning device in the South. This venture was a failure, and a year later he, his wife, and their four sons went to New York. The Smiths were accepted in literary circles and found no difficulty in publishing their writings in prominent reviews. From 1843 to 1845 Smith edited a New York daily, and two weeklies. For the next fifteen years he edited various publications, and founded his own magazine, *The Great Republic,* which lasted one year. He then retired to Patchogue, Long Island, where he died in 1868.

Smith was more than a political satirist—he was the literary progenitor of characters such as "Sam Slick," the Yankee peddler; "Artemus Ward," the illiterate but shrewd commentator on current events; and "Hosea Biglow," who flayed Northern and Southern politicians indiscriminately.

Upper Saddle River, N. J.
May, 1970

F. C. S.

MAJOR JACK DOWNING OF DOWNINGVILLE.

THE

SELECT LETTERS

OF

MAJOR JACK DOWNING,

OF THE DOWNINGVILLE MILITIA,

AWAY DOWN EAST, IN THE STATE OF MAINE.

WRITTEN BY HIMSELF.

Wonder of men ! like whom, to mortal eyes,
None e'er has risen, and none e'er shall rise,
How shall I fill a library with wit ?
When half the labour is unfinished yet,
They say, a fate attends on all I write,
And when I aim at praise they say I bite.
But rivals in pursuit of wealth, or fame,
To get an office, must obtain a name.

———

PHILADELPHIA,

PRINTED FOR THE PUBLISHER.

1834.

PREFASE.

SUM of the folks telld me that a prefase was of no use in this edishon of my letters, but I gues a book without a prefase is like a man without a head, and if a man wanted the head, every one knows what his boddy wud be wurth. But I want tu tell the folks jist this—There is a consarnt deal of letters pnblisht in my name. that arnt ginuin; so I've resolved tu print my rale ones, and lave out the counterfeits. I kinder feel tho, that so many attempts to imitate my letters is complimentary, as every one likes to rite letters in my name, and the nearer they cum tu the likeness the better they are. This is a sartan sine that I am popular, and that my day will cum as soon as the Ginerals is past. I have agreed tu publish this in Filadelfy, that I may have a chance to be more extensively known in the Key-stone-State where, I'm told they have nominated me, and where they are rale whalers of fellers for Dimocrasy and the Gineral, who never change a bit but remaines true Jacksonmen, in spite of all Jackson can do.

In this edishon I have put in my last letters. I wont tu sho that there's one man in the nation who is n't afeard tu spake his mind. I wont tu let the peeple see that I'm honest. and that if I'm elected, they will have a man, who never deals in Orakles,or abstroos metafisiks,sich as my opposer little Martin does, to sho his larnin and make folks scratch their heads whil readin tu understand him. I wont tu let them see tu, that I have ritin qualifikashons for a President, that I'm the rale stuff, and no slouch. If I'm tu be President, I wont the peeple tu be knowin in politiks, and be able tu fine out all my mistakes, bekase I'm a good republikin, and dont wont tu go rong any further than I can help; and when the peeple are knowin they will keep a good look out, tu see if I go rong

T 2

and tell me. I dont wont tu have all my own way, except n the vetoe, which is a consarnt good thing, as it keeps the Congress from duin foolish things, and I cant see what use the rite tu veto was put in the constitushon, if it wasn't tu use it on all okasions, and jest tu let the peeple see and feel the thority of the President. It is a kinder pulse, tu try by how far a President can go his own gate, and the peeple still cry hoorra.

This edishon has sum advantages over every other. It is selected with keer, and contains many important letters on the great consarns of the nashon, sent to the Portland Currier, and my friend Dwight of New York, and is, therefore, by far, the best Edishon yet publisht. I've made the publisher print it so that it'll cum cheap, that in these hard times, every one may have a coppy without much expense.

JACK DOWNING,

Downingville, *Jan.* 30. 1834.

CONTENTS.

MY GINUWINE LETTERS.

LETTER I.

Wherein is contained some account of Mr. Downing's
ancestors.

From the New York Daily Advertiser.

THE DOWNINGS.—The celebrity of Major Jack Downing has created an intense and very natural curiosity in
the public mind to know something of his origin and
ancestry. Hoping that some of the down-east antiqua-
ries and genealogists will favour the world with the in-
formation desired, I submit to your disposal the following imperfect notice of Sir George Downing, one of the
Major's ancestors, which I have drawn from an interest-
ing and learned work now in a course of publication, in
numbers, entitled 'Memorial of the Graduates of Harvard University, in Cambridge, Mass. Commencing
with the first class, 1642. By John Farmer, Cor. Sec.
of the N. H. Hist. Society.'

George Downing was born in London in 1624, and
accompanied his parents to this country when about
thirteen years of age. His father, Emanual Downing, a
great friend of New England, was brother-in-law to
John Winthrop, one of the principal founders and first
governor of Massachusetts. George received his edu-

A

cation at Harvard College. About 1646 he returned to England, when he was soon brought into notice, being, as Gov. Winthrop says, ' a very able scholar, and of ready wit and fluent utterance.' He was appointed chaplain in the regiment of Col. John Okey, in the army of Lord Fairfax, who had command of the Parliament forces in the north. In 1653 he was commissary general, and about the same time scout-master-general of the English army in Scotland. In the same year he was employed in negotiations with the Duke of Savoy. He seems to have been fitted by nature for scenes of political manœuvering ; and his principles were of such flexible character, that he could easily accommodate them to any service which the times required.

In 1655 he visited the French king on public business, and communicated his instructions in Latin. In 1657 he was appointed minister to Holland. In March, 1662, while in that country, in order to show his zeal and love for his majesty, he procured the arrest of John Okey, Miles Corbet, and John Barkstead, three of the Judges who had condemned to death Charles I, and sent them to England for trial. Okey had been the friend of Downing, who served in his regiment as chaplain. With the other two, he had co-operated in the cause of the Parliament. His conduct, therefore, in this transaction was justly reprobated.

He also spake of Cromwell as a traitor and rebel. In 1663, he was created a baronet. He informed Pepys that, when in Holland, ' he had so good spys, that he hath had the keys taken out of De Witt's (the Dutch minister) pocket when he was abed, and his closet opened and papers brought to him and left in his hands for an hour, and carried back and laid in the place again, and the keys put into his pocket. He says he hath had their most private debates, that have been between but two or three of them, brought to him, and in an hour after that hath sent word thereof to the king.' In 1671, he was again sent to Holland, but returning before he had executed the business of his mission to the satisfaction of the king, was imprisoned in the tower. He was afterwards restored to royal favour. In the difficulties which the New England colonies had with Charles II, from 1669, Mr. Downing was represented as having been very friendly to Massachusetts. He died in 1684 at the age of 60.

Major Jack Downing, of Downingville, seems to have inherited his distinguished ancestor's talents for war, business, and diplomacy, and, like him, to possess ready wit and fluent utterance, and to bask in the sunshine of royal favour. Whether he resembles him in other respects, time must disclose.

LETTER II.

Mr. Downing describes the method of making a Speaker.

Portland, Monday, Jan. 18, 1830.

To Cousin Ephraim Downing up in Downingville.

DEAR COUSIN EPHRAIM.—I now take my pen in hand to let you know that I am well, hoping these few lines will find you enjoying the same blessing. When I come down to Portland I did n't think o' staying more than three or four days, if I could sell my load of ax handles, and mother's cheese, and cousin Nabby's bundle of footings ; but when I got here I found uncle Nat was gone a freighting down to Quoddy, and ant Sally said as how I should n't stir a step home till he came back agin, which wont be this month. So here I am, loitering about this great town, as lazy as an ox. Ax handles dont fetch nothing, I could n't hardly give 'em away. Tell cousin Nabby I sold her footings for nine-pence a pair, and took it all in cotton cloth. Mother's cheese come to five-and-sixpence ; I got her a pound of shushon, and two ounces of snuff, and the

rest in sugar. When uncle Nat comes home I shall
put my ax handles aboard of him, and let him take 'em
to Boston next time he goes ; I saw a feller tother day,
that told me they'd fetch a good price there. I've been
here now a whole fortnight, and if I could tell ye one
half I've seen, I guess you'd stare worse than if you'd
seen a catamount. I've been to meeting, and to the
museum, and to both Legislaters, the one they call the
House, and the one they call the Sinnet. I spose
uncle Joshua is in a great hurry to hear something about
these Legislaters ; for you know he's always reading
newspapers, and talking politics, when he can get any
body to talk with him. I've seen him, when he had
five tons of hay in the field well made, and a heavy
shower coming up, stand two hours disputing with
squire W. about Adams and Jackson, one calling
Adams a tory and a fed, and the other saying Jackson
was a murderer and a fool ; so they kept it up, till the
rain began to pour down, and about spoilt all his hay.
Uncle Joshua may set his heart at rest about the
bushel of corn that he bet long with the post-master,
that Mr. Ruggles would be Speaker of that Legislater,
they call the House ; for he 's lost it, slick as a whistle. As I had n't much to do, I 've been there every
day since they 've been a setting. A Mr. White of
Monmouth was the Speaker the two first days ; and I
cant see why they did n't keep him in all the time ;
for he seemed to be a very clever good-natured sort of
man, and he had such a smooth pleasant way with him,
that I could n't help feeling sorry when they turned
him out and put in another. But some said he was n't
put in hardly fair ; and I dont know as he was, for the
first day when they were all coming in and crowding
round, there was a large fat man, with a round, full,
jolly sort of face, I suppose he was the captain, for he
got up and commanded them to come to order, and
then he told this Mr. White to whip into the chair
quicker than you could say Jack Robinson. Some
of 'em scolded about it, and I heard some, in a little

room they called the lobby, say 'twas a mean trick ; but
I could n't see why, for I thought Mr. White made a
capital Speaker, and when *our* company turns out you
know the captain always has a right to do as he's a
mind to.

They kept disputing most all the time the two first
days about a poor Mr. Roberts from Waterborough.—
Some said he should n't have a seat, because he adjourned the town meeting, and was n't fairly elected.—
Others said it was no such thing, and that he was elected as fairly as any of 'em. And Mr. Roberts himself
said he was, and said he could bring men that would
swear to it, and good men too. But notwithstanding
all this, when they came to vote, they got three or four
majority that he should n't have a seat. And I thought
it a needless piece of cruelty, for they want crowded,
and there was a number of seats empty. But they
would have it so, and the poor man had to go and stand
up in the lobby.

Then they disputed awhile about a Mr. Fowler's having a seat. Some said he should n't have a seat, because when he was elected some of his votes were
given for his father. But they were more kind to him
than they were to Mr. Roberts ; for they voted that he
should have a seat ; and I suppose it was because they
thought he had a lawful right to inherit whatever was
his father's. They all declared there was no party
politics about it, and I dont think there was ; for I noticed that all who voted that Mr. Roberts *should* have
a seat, voted that Mr. Fowler should *not* ; and all who
voted that Mr. Roberts should *not* have a seat, voted
that Mr. Fowler *should.* So, as they all voted *both*
ways, they must have acted as their consciences told
them, and I dont see how there could be any party
about it.

It 's a pity they could n't be allowed to have two
speakers, for they seemed to be very anxious to choose
Mr. Ruggles and Mr. Goodenow. They two had every vote, except one, and if they had had *that,* I be-

A2

lieve they would both have been chosen ; as it was,
however, they both came within a humbird's eye of it.
Whether it was Mr. Ruggles that voted for Mr. Goodenow, or Mr. Goodedow for Mr. Ruggles, I cant exactly tell ; but I rather guess it was Mr. Ruggles voted for Mr. Goodenow, for he appeared to be very glad
that Mr. Goodenow was elected, and went up to him
soon after Mr. Goodenow took the chair, and shook
hands with him as good-natured as could be.   I would
have given half my load of ax handles, if they could
both have been elected and set up there together, they
would have been so happy.   But as they can't have but
one speaker at a time, and as Mr. Goodenow appears
to understand the business very well, it is not likely
Mr. Ruggles will be speaker any this winter.   So uncle
Joshua will have to shell out his bushel of corn, and I
hope it will learn him better than to bet about politics
again.   If he had not been a goose, he might have
known he would loose it, even if he had been ever so
sure of getting it ; for in these politics there's never
any telling which way the cat will jump.   You know,
before the last September election, some of the papers
that came to our town had found out that *Mr. Hunton*
would have five thousand majority of the votes.   And
some of the other papers had found out that *Mr. Smith*
would have five thousand majority.   But the cat jumped 'tother way to *both* of 'em ; for I cant find yet as
either of 'em got *any* majority.   Some say Mr. Hunton has got a *little* majority, but as far from five thousand as I am from home.   And as for Mr. Smith, they
dont think he has any majority at all.   You remember,
too, before I came from home, some of the papers said
how there was a majority of ten or fifteen *national republicans* in the Legislater, and the other papers said
there was a pretty clever little majority of *democratic
republicans*.   Well, now every body says it has turned
out jest as that queer little paper, called the Daily
Courier, said 't would.   That paper said it was such a
close rub, it could n't hardly tell which side would beat.

And it 's jest so, for they've been here now most a fortnight acting jest like two boys playin see-saw on a rail. First one goes up, then 'tother ; but I reckon one of the boys is rather heaviest, for once in awhile he comes down chuck, and throws the other up into the air as though he would pitch him head over heels.

In that 'tother Legislator they call the Sinnet, there has been some of the drollest carryins on that you ever heard of. If I can get time I'll write you something about it, pretty soon. So I subscribe myself, in haste, your loving cousin till death.

JACK DOWNING.

LETTER III.

Uncle Joshua's visit to Boston, and dines with the Gineral Court

DEAR NEFFU,—I left home just after your letter to your cousin Ephraim got there, and I did'nt get a sight of your letter to me that you put in the Courier at Portland, until I saw it in the Daily Advertiser in Boston, and I guess Mr. Hale is the only person in Boston who takes that are little Courier, so you was pretty safe about the letter not being seen, as the printer promised you.—How I happened to see it here, you will find out before I have got through with this letter. I guess you wont be a little struck up when you find out that I'm in Boston—but I had best begin at the beginning and then I shall get thro' quicker.

After seeing your letter to Ephraim as I said before, I concluded it would'nt be a bad scheme to tackle up and take a load of turkies, some apple-sauce, and other notions that the neighbors wanted to get to market, and as your uncle Nat would be in Boston with the ax handles, we all thought best to try our luck there. Nothing happened worth mentioning on the road, nor till next

morning after I got here and put up in Elm street.
I then got off my watch pretty curiously, as you shall
be informed. I was down in the bar room, and tho't it
well enough to look pretty considerable smart, and now
and then compared my watch with the clock in the bar
and found it as near right as ever it was—when a feller
stept up to me and ask't how I'd trade? and says I, for
what? and says he for your watch—and says I, any
way that will be a fair shake—upon that says he, I'll
give you *my* watch and five dollars—Says I, its done!
He gave me the five dollars, and I gave him my watch.
Now, says I, give me *your* watch—and says he, with a
loud laugh, I han't got none—and that kind aturn'd
the laugh on me. Thinks I, let them laugh that lose.
Soon as the laugh was well over, the feller thought he'd
try the watch to his ear—why, says he, it dont go—no,
says I, not without its carried—then I began to laugh—
he tried to open it and could'nt start it a hair, and broke
his thumb nail into the bargain. Won't she open, says
he? Not's I know on, says I—and then the laugh
seemed to take onother turn.

Don't you think I got off the old Brittannia pretty
well, considerin? And then I thought I'd go and see
about my load of turkies and other notions. I expected
to have gone all over town to sell my load, but Mr.
Doolittle told me if I'd go down to the new market, I
should find folks enough to buy all I had at once. So
down I goes, and a likely kind of a feller, with an eye
like a hawk and quick as a steeltrap for a trade, (they
called him a 4th staller,) came up to the wagon, and
before you could say Jack Robinson, we struck a bargain for the whole cargo—and come to weigh and reckon up, I found I should get as much as 10s6d more than
any of us calculated before I left home, and had the apple-sauce left besides. So I thought I'd jist see how
this 4th staller worked his card to be able to give us so
good a price for the turkies, and I went inside the mar-
ket-house, and a grander sight I never expect to see!
But it was the 3d staller instead of the 4th, had my tur-

kies all sorted and hung up, and looking so much better that I hardly should know 'em. Pretty soon, a gentleman asked the 3d staller what he asked for turkies ? Why, says he, if you want something better than you ever saw before, there's some 'twas killed last night purpose for you. You may take 'em at 9d, being it's you. I'll give you 12 cents, said the gentleman, as I've got some of the General Court to dine with me, and must treat well. I shant stand for half a cent with an old customer, says he. And so they traded ; and in about the space of half an hour or more, all my turkies went into baskets at that rate. The 4th staller gave me 6d a pound, and I began to think I'd been a little too much in a hurry for trade—but's no use to cry for spilt milk. Then I went up to the State House to see what was going on there ; but I thought I'd get off my apple-sauce on my way—and seeing a sign of old clothes bartered, I stepped in and made a trade, and got a whole suit of superfine black broadcloth from top to toe, for a firkin of apple-sauce, (which didn't cost much I guess, at home.)

Accordingly I rigged myself up in the new suit, and you'd hardly known me. I didn't like the set of the shoulders, they were so dreadful puckery ; but the man said that was all right. I guess he'll find the apple-sauce full as puckery when he gets down into it—but that's between ourselves. Well, when I got up to the State House I found them at work on the rail road— busy enough I can tell you—they got a part of it made already. I found most all the folks kept their hats on except the man who was talking out loud and the man he was talking to—all the rest seemed to be busy about their own consarns. As I didn't see any body to talk to I kept my hat on and took a seat, and look'd round to see what was going on. I hadn't been setting long before I saw a slick-headed, sharp-eyed little man, who seemed to have the principal management of the folks, looking at me pretty sharp, as much as to say who are you ? but I said nothing and looked tother way—at last he touched me on the shoulder—I thought he was feel-

ing of the puckers. Are you a member ? says he—sartin says I—how long have you taken your seat ? says
he. About ten minutes, says I. Are you qualified ?
says he. I guess not, says I. And then he left me.
I didn't know exactly what this old gentleman was after—but soon he returned and said it was proper for
me to be qualified before I took a seat, and I must go
before the governor! By Jing! I never felt so before
in oll my born days. As good luck would have it, he
was beckoned to come to a man at the desk, and as soon
as his back was turned I give him the slip. Jest as I
was going off, the gentleman who bought my turkies of
the 4th staller took hold of my arm, and I was afraid at
first that he was going to carry me to the Governor—
but he began to talk as sociable as if we had been old
acquaintances. How long have you been in the house,
Mr. Smith, says he. My name is Downing, said I.
I beg your pardon, says he—I mean Downing. It's no
offence, says I, I hav'nt been here long. Then says he
in a very pleasant way, a few of your brother members
are to take pot-luck with me to-day, and I should be very happy to have you join them. What's pot-luck said
I. O, a family dinner, says he—no ceremony. I
thought by this time I was well qualified for that without going to the Governor. So says I, yes, and thank
ye too. How long before you'll want me, says I. At
3 o'clock, says he, and gave me a piece of paste board
with his name on it—and the name of the street, and
the number of his house, and said that would show me
the way. Well, says I, I dont know of nothing that
will keep me away, And then we parted. I took considerable liking to him.

After strolling round and seeing a great many things
about the 'State House and the marble image of Gin.
Washington, standing on a stump in the Porch, I went
out into the street they call Bacon street, and my stars !
what swarms of women folks I saw all drest up as if
they were going to meetin. You can tell cousin Polly
Sandburn, who you know is no slimster, that she needn't

take on so about being genteel in her shapes—for the genteelest ladies here beat her as to size all hollow. I dont believe one of 'em could get into our fore dore—and as for their arms—I shouldn't want better measure for a bushel of meal than one of their sleeves could hold. I shant shell out the bushel of corn you say I've lost on Speaker Ruggles at that rate. But this puts me in mind of the dinner which Mr. ———— wants I should help the Gineral Court eat. So I took out the piece of paste board, and began to inquire my way and got along completely, and found the number the first time—but the door was locked, and there was no knocker, and I I thumpt with my whip handle, but nobody come. And says I to a man going by, dont nobody live here? and says he yes. Well, how do you get in? Why, says he, ring; and says I, ring what? And says he, the bell. And says I where's the rope? And says he, pull that little brass nub: and so I gave it a twitch, and I'm sure a bell did ring; and who do you think opened the door with a white apron afore him? You couldn't guess for a week a Sundays—so I'll tell you. It was Stephen Furlong, who kept our district school last winter, for 5 dollars a month, and kept bachelor's hall, and helped tend for Gineral Coombs a training days, and make out muster rolls. We was considerably struck up at first, both of us; and when he found I was going to eat dinner with Mr. ———— and Gineral Court, he thought it queer kind of doings—but says he, I guess it will be as well for both of us not to know each other a bit more than we can help. And says I, with a wink, you're half right, and in I went. There was nobody in the room but Mr. ———— and his wife, and not a sign of any dinner to be seen any where—though I thought now and then when a side door opened, I could smell cupboard, as they say.

I thought I should be puzzled enough to know what to say, but I hadn't my thoughts long to myself. Mr. ———— has about as nimble a tongue as you ever heard, and could say ten words to my one, and I had nothing

to do in the way of making talk. Just then I heard a
ringing, and Stephen was busy in opening the door and
letting in the Gineral Court. who all had their hats off,
and looking pretty scrumptious, you may depend. I
did'nt see but I could stand along side of 'em without
disparagement, except to my boots, which had just got
a lick of beeswax and tallow—not a mite of dinner yet,
and I began to feel as if 'twas nearer supper time than
dinner time—when all at once two doors flew away from
each other right into the wall, and what did I see but
one of the grandest thanksgiving dinners you ever laid
your eyes on—and lights on the table, and silver can-
dlesticks and gold lamps over head—the window shut-
ters closed—I guess more than one of us stared at first,
but we soon found the way to our mouths—I made Stephen tend out for me pretty sharp, and he got my plate
filled three or four times with soup, which beat all I ever
tasted. I shan't go through the whole dinner again to
you—but I am mistaken if it cost me much for victuals
this week, if I pay by the meal at Mr. Doolittle's, who
comes pretty near up to a thanksgiving every day.
There was considerable talk about stock and manufac-
tories, and lier bilities, and rimidies, and a great loss
on stock. I thought this a good chance for me to put
in a word—for I calculated I knew as much about rais-
ing stock and keeping over as any of 'em. Says I to
Mr. ——, there's one thing I've always observed in
my experience in stock—just as sure as you try to keep
over more stock than you have fodder to carry them
well into April, one half will die on your hands, to a
sartinty—and there's no remedy for it—I've tried it
out and out, and there's no law that can make a ton of
hay keep over ten cows, unless you have more carrots
and potatoes than you can throw a stick at. This made
some of the folks stare who didn't know much about
stock—and Steve give me a jog, as much as to say, keep
quiet. He thought I was getting into a quog-mire, and
soon after, giving me a wink, opened the door and got
me out of the room into the entry.

After we had got out of hearing, says I to Steve, how are you getting on in the world—should you like to come back to keep our school if I could get a vote for you!—not by two chalks, says Steve—I know which side my bread is buttered better than all that—I get 12 dollars a month and found, and now and then some old clothes, which is better than keeping school at 5 dollars and find myself, and work out my highway tax besides—then turning up the cape of my *new coat*, says he, I guess I've dusted that afore now—most likely, says I, but not in our district school. And this brings to mind to tell you how I got a sight of your letter. They tell me here that every body reads the Boston Daily Advertiser, because there is no knowing but what they may find out something to their advantage, so I thought I would be as wise as the rest of them, and before I got half through with it, what should I find mixed up among the news but your letter that you put into that little paper down in Portland, and I knew it was your writing before I had read ten lines of it.

I hope I've answered it to your satisfaction.

Your respected uncle, JOSHUA DOWNING.

P. S. Mr. Topliff says your uncle Nat is telegraphed, but I'm afraid the ax handles wont come to much—I find the Boston folks made a handle of most any thing they can lay hold of, and just as like as not they'll make a handle of our private letters, if they should see them.

N. B. You spell dreadful bad, according to my notion—and this proves what I always said, that our district has been going down hill ever since Stephen Furlong left it.

B

LETTER IV.

*Mr. Downing relates the scrape the legislature got into,
in trying to make a number of governors.*

Portland, Feb. 1, 1830.

To Cousin Ephraim Downing up in Downingville.

DEAR COUSIN EPHRAIM.—I spose you expected me
to write to you agin long afore now and tell you something more about these legislaters, and I meant to, but I
could n't very well ; for I'll tell you jest how twas.—
Some days, when the legislater would get into a plaguy
hobble, I would think to myself, well, soon as they get
out of this snarl, I'll write to cousin Ephraim and tell
him all about it ; but before they got fairly out of that,
they'd be right into another ; and if I waited till next
day to see how that ended, my keesers! before night
they'd all be higgeldy piggle in a worse hobble than
they'd ever been in afore. So if I wait to tell you how
it comes out, I believe I shall have to wait till haying
time.   Another thing I've been waiting for, was to tell
you who was Governor.   But, O dear, I cant find out
half so much about it now, here in this great city of
Portland, where all the Governors live, as I could six
months ago among the bear traps and log houses in our
town, way back into the woods. Last August, you know,
according to the papers we were going to have two
Governors right off, sure as rates ; Mr. Hunton and Mr.
Smith.   Well now its got to be the first of February,
and we haven't got *one* yet.   And although the governor-
makers have had four or five under way for a month
past, some think it very doubtful whether they will get
one done so as to be fit to use this year.   There's Mr.
Hunton, and Mr. Smith, and Mr. Cutler, and Mr.
Goodenow, and Mr. Hall, have all been *partly* made
into Governors ; but when in all creation any of 'em
will be *finished*, I guess it would puzzle a Philadelphy
lawyer to tell.   I stated in my letter to uncle Joshua,

that there were two very clever parties in the legislater, the democratic republikans and the national republikans ; and they are so, and very industrious, and try to make things go on right ; and I really believe, if the confounded Jacksonites and Huntonites didn't bother 'em so, they'd make us a Governor, as quick as I could make an ax handle. It is enough to do any body's heart good to see how kind and obliging these democratic republikans and national republikans are to each other, and how each party tries to help the other along; and its enough to make any body's blood boil to see the Jacksonites and Huntonites, jest like the dog in the manger, because they cant eat the hay themselves, snap at these two clever parties the moment either of 'em sets out to take a mouthful. I'll jest give you an instance of the kindness that these two clever parties show to each other. You know the constitution says when we haven't any Governor the President of the Sinnet must be Governor, and when we have n't any President of the Sinnet, the Speaker of the House must be Governor. So when Governor Lincoln died Mr. Cutler was Governor for awhile, because he was last year President of the Sinnet. Mr. Goodenow is a national republikan, and when he was elected Speaker of the House, the democratic republikans told him as there was no President of the Sinnet elected yet, it belonged to him to be Governor, and tried as hard as though he had belonged to their own party, to encourage him to go right into the council chamber and do the governor's business. But the national republikans didn't dare to let him go, for he was elected by only one majority, and they said if he should leave the chair, it wouldn't be five minutes before a Jacksonite would be whisked into it, and then the two clever parties would all be up a tree. Well, jest so twas in the Sinnet after Elder Hall was elected president, only the bread was buttered on tother side. Elder Hall is a democrat republikan, and there was a great deal tougher scrabble to elect him, than there was to choose the Speaker of the

House. But as soon as he was elected, the national republikans went to him very kindly, and said, 'Elder Hall, by the provisions of the constitution you are now fairly Governor of the State till another governor is qualified. Dont be bashful about it, but please to walk right into the Council chamber, and do the governor's business.' But the democratic republikans said, that would never do, for if he should, the Sinnet Board would be capsized in an instant and the Huntonites would rule the roast. So there was a pair of Governors spoilt when they were more than half made, jest by the mischief of the Jacksonites and Huntonites. And the consequence is, that Mr. Cutler has to keep doing the Governor's business yet, whether he wants to or not, and whether it is right for him to, or not. They say the poor man is a good deal distressed about it, and has sent to the great Judges of the Supreme Court to know whether it's right for him to be Governor any longer or not. If the Judges should say he mus 'nt be Governor any longer, we shall be in a dreadful pickle. Only think, no Governor, and no laws, but every body do jest as they're a mind to. Well, if that should be the case, I know one thing, that is, Bill Johnson will get one good flogging for calling me a mean puppy and a coward last summer ; I've longed to give it to him ever since ; and if the Legislater don't make a governor this winter, I shall come right home, and Bill must look out. What a pity 'tis they should waste so much time trying to make so many governors ; for, if they should make a dozen, we shouldn't want to use but one this year ; and it is thought if they had all clapt to and worked upon one instead of working upon so many, they might have had him done more than three weeks ago.

Your lovin cuzen til death,

JACK DOWNING.

LETTER V.

Mr. Downing describes the predicament in which the house of Representatives got into.

Portland, Tuesday, Feb. 2, 1830.

DEAR COUSIN EPHRAIM,—I have just time to write you a short *postscript* to a letter that I shall send you in a day or two. We have had a dreadful time here to-day. You know the wheels of government have been stopt here for three or four weeks, and they all clapt their shoulders under to-day, and give 'em a lift ; and they started so hard, that as true as you're alive, *they split both Legislaters right in tu.* Some say they are split so bad, they can't mend 'em again, but I hope they can though ; I shall tell you all about how 'twas done, in a day or two. I've been expecting a letter from you, or some of the folks, sometime. As I've got prerty short of money, I wish you would send 'em in the *Daily Courier*, so I shant have to pay the postage.

Your hearty cousin,
JACK DOWNING.

LETTER VI.

In which things look brighter.

Portland, Feb. 3, 1830.

COUSIN EPHRAIM,—I thought I would jest write you another little *postscript* to my letter that I was going to send you in a day or tu, and let you know that the legislaters want split so bad as some folks tho't for.— They've got 'em both mended agin, so that they set 'em agoing to day afore noon. But in the arternoon, that legislater they call the Sinnet, got struck, and in try-

B 2

ing to make it go, it rather seemed to crack a little;
so they stopt short till to-morrow. Its been jostled
about so, and got so weak an' rickety, some are afraid
it will give out yet, or *split in tu agin.*

                                JACK DOWNING.

LETTER VII.

*An account of the trigging of the wheels of govern-
ment.*

                Portland, Thursday Feb. 11, 1831.

DEAR COUSIN EPHRAIM.—I've wrote you three *post-
scripts* since I wrote you a letter, and the reason is,
these Legislaters have been carryin on so like all pos-
sest, and I've been in looking at 'em so much, I could
n't get time to write more than three lines at once, for
fear I should be out of the way, and should miss seeing some of the fun. But thinkin you'd be tired of
waiting, I tried to get the printer to send my letter yesterday; but he told me right up and down he could n't.
I told him he must, for I ought to sent before now.—
But he said he could n't and would n't, and that was
the upshot of the matter, for the paper was chock full,
and more tu, of the Governor's message. Bless my
stars, says I, and have we got a Governor done enough
so he can speak a message? Yes, indeed we have,
says he, *thanks be to the two great republikin parties,*
who have saved the State from the anarkee of the Jacksonites and Huntonites; the Governor is done, and is
jest a going into the Lesislater, and if you 'll go right
up there, you can see him. So I pushed in among the
crowd, and I got a pretty good squeezin tu; but I got
a good place, for I could elbow it as well as any on 'em.
And I had n't been there five minutes, seemingly, before we had a Governor sure enough; and a good stout,

genteel looking sort of a man he was tu, as you would see in a whole regiment, taking in captains and all.— Nobody disputed that he was finished pretty workmanlike ; and he ought to be, for they 'd been long enough about it. So they concluded to swear him in, as they call it, and he took a great oath to behave like a Governor a whole year. Some say the wheels of government will go along smooth and easy now, as a wheelbarrow across a brick yard ; but some shake their heads, and say the wheels will be jolting over rocks and stumps all winter yet ; and I dont know but they will, for the Governor had n't hardly turned his back upon 'em and gone out, before they went right to disputing agin as hard as ever. I was a good mind to run out and call the Governor back to still 'em. But I could n't tell where to look for him, so they got clear of a drubbing that time. I know he 'd a gin it to 'em if he 'd been there ; for what do you think was the first thing they went to disputing about ? It was how many Governor's speeches they should print this winter ; jest as if the Governor could n't tell that himself. Some wanted three hundred, and some five hundred, and some seven or eight hundred. Finally they concluded to print five hundred ; and I should think that was enough in all conscience, if they are all going to be as long as that one they printed in the Courier yesterday. In the next place, they took up that everlasting dispute about Mr. Roberts' having a seat; for if you 'll believe me, they've kept that poor man standing there till this time.

I'll tell you how tis, Cousin Ephraim, we must contrive some way or other to keep these Jacksonites and Huntonites out of the Legislater another year, or we shall be ruin'd ; for they make pesky bad work, triging the wheels of government. They 've triged 'em so much that they say it has cost the State about *fifteen thousand dollars* a'ready, more than 'twould, if they had gone along straight without stopping. So you may tell uncle Joshua that besides that bushel of corn he lost in betting about the Speaker, he'll have to shell out as

much as *two bushels more* to pay the cost of triging the
wheels. Jingoe! sometimes when I've seen the wheels
chocked with a little trig not bigger than a cat's head,
and the whole legislater trying with all their might two
or three days, and couldn't start it a hair, how I've
longed to hitch on my little speckled four-year-olds,
and give 'em a pull ; if they wouldn't make the wheels
fly over the trigs in a jiffy, I wont guess agin. 'Tother
day in a great convention, when both Legislaters met
together to chuse some Counsellors, Mr. Boutelle and
Mr. Smith of Nobleborough tried to explain how 'twas
the wheels of government were trig'd so much. Mr.
Boutelle, as I have told you a-fore, is a national republican, and Mr. Smith is a democratic republican.—
They differed a little in their opinion. Mr. Boutelle
seemed to think the trigs were all put under by *one class
of politicians*, and from what he said, I took it he meant
the Jacksonites. He said ever since the Legislater began, the moment they staited the wheels, that class of
politicians would throw under a chock and stop 'em ;
and which ever way they turned, that class of politicians would meet 'em at every corner and bring 'em up
all standin. Mr. Smith seemed to think *another* class
of politicians had the greatest hand in it, and it was
pretty clear he meant the Huntonites. He said when
they first got here, that class of politicians sot the
wheels of government rolling the *wrong way;* they put
the big wheels forward, and the Legislater had been
going backwards ever since, just like a lobster. And
the Huntonites not only trig'd, the wheels, whenever
they begun to roll the right way ; but as soon as the
'blessed Governor' was done they trig'd him tu ; and
though he had been done four days, they would'nt let
him come into the Legislater so that their eyes could
be blest with the sight of him. So from what I can
find out, the Jacksonites and Huntonites both, are a
troublesome contrary set, and there must be some way
contrived to keep 'em out of the Legislater in future.

It seems soon after you got my first letter, uncle

Joshua tackled up, and started off to Boston with a load of turkeys and apple-sauce. I had a letter from him t'other day, as long as all out doors, in the Boston Advertiser. He says he got more for the turkeys than he expected tu ; but I think its a plaguy pity he did'nt bring 'em to Portland. I know he'd got more than he could in Boston. Provision kind is getting up here wonderfully, on account of these Legislaters being likely to stay here all winter ; and some think the'll be here half the summer tu. And then there's sich a cloud of what they call lobby members and office hunters, that the butchers have got frightened, and gone to buying up all the beef and pork they can get hold on far and near for they are afraid a famine will be upon us next. Howsomever, uncle Joshua did well to carry his 'puckery apple-sauce' to Boston. He could n't get a cent for't here ; for every body's puckery and soar enough here now.

Give my love to father and mother and cousin Nabby. I shall answer their letters as soon as I can.

Your lovin Cousin,

JACK DOWNING.

LETTER VIII.

Mr. Downing advises his uncle Joshua to hold on to his bushel of corn as the legislature had undertaken " to rip up their duins."

Portland, Friday, Feb. 12, 1830.

Postscript to uncle Joshua.

☞THIS WITH CARE AND SPEED.

DEAR UNCLE,—If you have'nt paid over that are bushel of corn yet, that you lost when you bet Mr. Ruggles would be Speaker, hold on to it for your life, till you hear from me agin, for I aint so clear but you may save it yet. They've gone to rippin up their duins here, and there's no knowing but they may go clear back to the beginning and have another tug about Speaker. At any rate, if your bushel of corn is'nt gone out of your crib yet, I advise you by all means to keep it there.

Tell 'squire N. the question is'nt settled yet; and you wont shell out a single kernel till it is fairly nailed and clinched, so it can't be ript up agin. I'll tell you what 'tis, uncle Josh, the Supreme Court beats the Jacksonites and Huntonites all hollow for trigging the wheels. You know after they had such a tussle for about a week to chose Elder Hall President of the Sinnet, and after he come in at last all hollow, for they said he had a majority of eight out of sixteen, they went on then two or three weeks nicely, duin business *tie and tie*, hard as they could. Then up steps the Judges of the Supreme Court and tells Mr. Hall he was governor, and ought to go into the Council Chamber. They seemed to be a little bit thunder struck at first. But they soon come to agin, and Elder Hall got out of the chair and Mr. Kingsbury got into it, and they jogged along another week, duin business as hard as ever. They said all the chairs round the table ought to be filled, so they changed works with the House and made four more Sinneters. So having four good fresh hands come in, they took hold in good earnest and turned off more business in two days, than they had done in a month before.

Then up steps the Supreme Court agin and tells 'em their cake is all dough; for they had n't been duin constitutional. This was yesterday; and it made a dreadful touse. They went right to work rippin up and tarrin away what they'd been duin; and before nine o'clock in the evening they turned out the four new Sinneters, out of their chairs and appointed a committee to begin to make four more. They took hold so hash about it, I spose some the rest of the Sinneters begun to be afraid they should be ript up tu; so they clear'd out, I guess

near about half on 'em, and have n't been seen nor heard
of to day. Some of 'em that had more courage went
in and tried to do business ; but there was n't enough of
'em to start an inch. They sent a man all around town
in the forenoon and afternoon to tell 'm to come in and
go to work, but he could n't find hide nor hair of one of
'em. Elder Hall said *he guessed they must be somewhere in a convention.*

Some say they'll rip up the new Councillors next, and
then the Governor, cause the new Sinneters helpt make
em all. But there's one comfort left for us, let the cat
jump which way 'twill ; if Mr. Hunton isn't a constitutional Governor, Elder Hall is ; the Judges have nailed
that fast. So think Bill Johnson will get off with a
whole skin, for I shant dare to flog him this year. If
they go clear back to the Speaker, and decide it in favor
of your bushel of corn, I shall let you know as soon as
possible.

Your lovin neffu,

JACK DOWNING.

LETTER IX.

The queer duins of the senate described.

To Cousin Ephraim Downing up in Downingville.

Portland, Wednesday, Feb. 17, 1830.

DEAR COUSIN EPHRAIM,—Here I am yet, and have
n't much else to du, so I might as well keep writin to
you ; for I spose uncle Joshua 's in a peck of trouble
about his bushel of corn. I'm pesky fraid he'll lose it
yet ; for they don't seem to rip up worth a cent since
the first night they begun. The truth was they took hold
rather tu hash that night ; and rippin up them are four
new Sinneters so quick, they scart away four or five

more old ones, so they didn't dare to come in again for
tu days· And that threw 'em all into the suds, head
and ears. It was worse than triging the wheels, for
it broke the Sinnet wheel right in tu, and left it so flat,
that all Job's oxen never could start it, if they hadn't
got it mended again. They tried, to keep duin something, but they couldn't du the leastest thing. One time
they tried to du something with a little bit of a message that was sent to 'em on a piece of paper from the
House. The President took it in his hand, and held
it up, and asked 'em what best to du with it. Some
of 'em motioned that they'd lay it on the table ; but
come to consider on it, they found they couldn't according to the constitution, without there was more of
'em to help. They said they couldn't lay it on the table, nor du nothin at all with it. I was afraid the poor
old gentleman would have to stand there and hold it
till they got the wheel mended agin. But I believe he
finally *let it drop* on the table ; and I spose there was
nothin in the constitution against that.

They got the wheel mended Monday about eleven er
clock, so they could start along a little. But them are
four new Sinneters that they ript up Thursday night,
come right back agin Monday, and sot down to the
great round table ; and stood tu it through thick and
thin, that they want rip up, and no sich thing. Well,
this kicked up a kind of a bobbery among 'em, so they
thought they'd try to journ. The President counted
'em, and said they were journed and might go out.
One of the new Sinneters said the President didn't count
right, and they want journed a bit ; and they must set
still and have an overhauling about it.

So they set down agin, all but four or five that put
on their hats and great coats and stood backside of the
room. The room was chock full of folks looking on,
and the President told 'em the Sinnet was journed and
they might as well go out, but they did seem to keer tu,
and they put their hats on and began to laugh like fun·
The President sot still in his cheer, for I spose he

thought if he left it, some of them are roguish fellers would be gettin into it. The man that keeps order, told the folks they must take their hats off when they were in the Sinnet ; but they said they wouldn't, cause the Sinnet was adjourned. Then the man went and asked the President if the Sinnet was all adjourned, and the President said 'twas, and there was no doubt about it. And the folks felt so tickled to think they could wear their hats when the Sinneters were setting round the great table, that they kind of whistled a little bit all over the room.

Finally, after settin about half an hour, another man got up and motioned to ajourn, and the President got up and put it to vote agin. He told 'em if they wanted to ajourn, they must say ah, and they all said ah this time, and cleared out in five minutes.

But about this rippin up business ; instead of rippin up the councillors, as some thought they would, both legislaters met together to-day, and called in four of the councillors, and nailed 'em down harder with an oath.

They've sot the committees to work like fun now, and its thought they'll turn off business hand over hand; for you know its almost March, and then the great Supreme Court meets here. And they say they have a grand jury that picks up all disorderly and mischievous folk, and carries 'em into court, and the court puts 'em in jail. These legislaters have been cuttin up such rigs here all winter, that they begin to look pretty shy when any thing is said about the first of March, and I dont believe the grand jury 'll be able to find a single mother's son of 'em when the court gets here.

From your cousin,
JACK DOWNING.

C

LETTER X.

*A new idea for making money out of the office seekers,
swarming round the new governor.*

Postscript to Ephraim.

Portland, Feb. 23, 1830.

DEAR COUSIN.—As soon as you get this, I want you
to load up tho old lumber-box with them are long slick
bean-poles, that I got out last summer. I guess I shant
make much by my ax handles, for I can't sell 'em yet;
I hant sold but tu since I've been here ; and the sea's
been froze over so that uncle Ned hant got in from
Quoddy yet, and I hant had any chance to send my ax
handles to Boston. But if I lose on the ax handles, I
shall make it up on the bean poles if you only get 'em
here in season. Do make haste as fast as you can, and
you shall share half the profits.

It ant to stick beans with nuther ; and I guess you'll
kind o' laff, when I tell you what tis for. You know
when we went to the court there was a man sot up in a
box, that they called a Sheriff, and held a long white
pole in his hand. Well I heard somebody say tother
day that there was more than a hundred folks here that
wanted to get a Sheriff's pole ; and I happened to think
that them are bean poles would make cute ones. But
you must get 'em afore the Governor makes his appint-
ments, or it'll be gone goose with us, about it, for we
could'nt sell more than half a dozen arter that.

From your Cousin,
JACK DOWNING.

LETTER XI.

Cousin Ephraim in the difficulties.

————— Feb. 25, 1830.

DEAR JACK.—Here I am, about half way to Portland,
with one shu of the old lumber box broke down, and

tother one putty rickety. Its about half the way bare ground, and the old hoss begins to be ruther wheezy. But you know I don't give up for trifles, when there's a chance to make a spec. Soon as I got your letter about the bean poles, I made business fly. Mother put me up a box of beef and dough nuts, and I fed old grey, and tackled up, and all loaded and ready to start in tu hours ; and if I live I shall get the bean poles there at some rate or other fore long ; but I'm fraid I may be late. If you know the Governor, I wish you'd just ask him to keep his appointments back a little while ; he shant loose nothing by it if the poles sell well. I shall have to go the rest of the way on wheels, and I want you to see if you can hire one of the government wheels and come and meet me, for the plaguy fellers here wont trust me with their wheels till I get back. Besides if I could get one of the wheels of government, I'm thinking I could get along a good deal faster ; for I met a man jest now from Portland that said they've got them are wheels going now like a buz. He said there was no wheels in the country that could go half so fast ; and he thinks they work a good deal better for being split up and mended so much. Grandfather said they would want as many cockades as Sheriff polls ; and so he put in his old continental one, that he had in the revolution.

P. S. I hope you'll get the government wheels to come arter the poles, for I want some that are putty easy *trig'd*, cause the hills are ruther slippery.

Your Cusin,

JACK DOWNING.

LETTER XII.

A tug at the wheels of government described.

Portland, March 3, 1830.

To Cousin Ephraim Downing, stuck by the way.

You sent word to me in your letter t'other day, that you had got to bare ground, and broke down one shu of the lumber box, and wanted me to get the wheels of Government and come up after the poles. I tried to get 'em, but they wouldn't let 'em go ; and they said 'twould'nt be any use if I did ; for I could'nt get more than ten rods before the wheels would be trig'd. They were expecting of 'em to be trig'd every day, they said ; for the Judges had sent a monstrous great trig to the Governor, and told him if they went to start the wheels forward any, he must clap it under ; for they must'nt go forward a bit more, and must roll the wheels back a good ways, till they find the right road. Well, sure enough, on Tuesday, when they was goin along a little easy, and some on 'em threw the trig right under, and it brought 'em up with a dreadful jolt.

And then, my stars, if the Sinneters didn't go at it tie and tie, like smoke. The national republicans pulled one way, and the democratic republicans 'tother, with all their might, jest as you and I used to set down and brace our feet against each other, and take hold of a stick to see which could pull tother up. They pulled and grinned all day, but nary side couldn't pull up tother. The national republicans said they wouldn't stop for that little trig, nor no notiou of it ; and they pulled the wheels forward as hard as they could. The democratic republicans braced their feet tother way, and said the wheels shouldn't move another inch forward ; they had got on to a wrong road, and the Judges had put that trig there to keep 'em all from goin to destruction ; and they tried all day as hard as they could to roll the wheels back to find the right road. They pulled like my little tu year olds all day, but I couldn't see as they started the wheels backwards or forwards a single hair. This morning they hitched on and took another jest sich a pull. The national republicans said they knew the road as well as the Judges did, and they were goin right and wouldn't touch to go back ; the road was a good plain smooth road, and there was'nt a mite of danger in goin on. The democratic republicans said they could hear some pretty heavy thundering along that road, and

tney'd not go another step that way ; bnt they stood tu
they want afraid of the thunder.   The national republicans said they'd heard thunder before now, and seen
dreadful black clouds all over the sky, and they'd seen
a fair afternoor and a bright rainbow after all that. So
they pulled and disputed, and disputed and pulled, till
most noon, and then they concluded to stop and breath
upon it till to-morrow, when I spose they will spit on
their hands to make 'em stick and begin as hard as ever.

I hope youl'll make haste and get the poles along ;
if you cant get any wheels up there, you better tie up a
couple of bundles of 'em and swing 'em across the old
horse, saddle-bag fashion.   You'll get well paid for it,
if you get 'em here in season.   Your cousin,
                                           JACK DOWNING.

<hr />

LETTER XIII.

*Mr. Downing tells what setting up a candidate for
affice means.*

Portland, Tuesday, March 16, 1830.

To Uncle Joshua Downing, up in Downingville.

DEAR UNCLE JOSHUA—I guess by this time, its so
long since I writ home, you almost begin to think Jack
is sick or dead, or gone down to Quoddy long with uncle
Nat, or somewhere else.   But you needn't think any
sich thing, for here I am sticking to Portland like wax,
and I guess I shant pull up stakes agin this one while.
The more I stay to Portland the better I like it.   Its a
nation fine place ; there's things enough here for any
body to see all their life time.   I guess I shall tell you
something about 'em before summer's out.   These Legislaters havn't done nothin scarcely worth telling about
this most a fortnight.   I've been in most every day jest
to take a squint at 'em.   There was n't hardly a bit of
a quarrel to be heard of from one day's end to an-
                                                C 2

other. They were all as good natured and loving as a family of brothers, that had been living out all summer, and had jest got home together at thanksgiving time. They kept to work as busy as bees upon pieces of paper that they called Bills. Sometimes they voted to read 'em once, sometimes twice, and sometimes three times. At last the sun begun to shine so warm, that it made 'em think of planting time, and at it they went, passing Bills *by the gross*, [probably a mistake for *to be engrossed*— editor,] till they settled 'em away like heaps of corn at a husking, before a barnful of boys and gals. And they've got so near the bottom of the heap, they say they shall brush out the floors in a day or two more, and start off home. I spose they wont mind it much if they do brush out some of the ears without husking; they've had their frolic and their husking supper, and I guess that's the most they come for. It seems to me, uncle Joshua, it costs our farmers a great deal more to husk out their law-corn every winter than it need tu. They let tu many noisy talking fellers come to the husking. I've always minded, when I went to a husking, that these noisy kind of chaps seems to care a good deal more about what they can get to eat and drink, than they du about the corn; and them are that don't make much fuss, are apt to husk the most and make the cleanest work.

O dear, uncle, there's a hot time ahead. I almost dread to think of it. I'm afraid there is going to be a worse scrabble next summer to see who shall go to the great State husking than there was last. The Hunton- ites and Smithites are determined to have each of 'em a governor agin next year. They've sot up their candi- dates on both sides ;' and who in all the world should you guess they are? The Huntonites have sot up Mr. Hunton, and the Smithites have sot up Mr. Smith. You understand what it means, I spose, to set up a candi- date. It means the same that it does at a shooting match to set up a goose or a turkey to be fired at. The rule of the game is that the Smithites are to fire at Mr.

Hunton, and the Huntonites are to fire at Mr. Smith.
They think it will take a pretty hard battle to get them
both in. But both parties say they've got the constitution on their side, so I think likely they'll both beat.

They've been piling up a monstrous heap of amuni-
tion this winter, enough to keep 'em firing all summer;
and I guess it wont be long before you see the smoke
rising all over the State, wherever there's a newspaper.
I think these newspapers are dreadful smoky things;
they are enough to blind any body's eyes any time. I
mean all except the *Daily Courier* and *Family Reader,*
that I send my letters in; I never see much smoke in
them. But take the rest of the papers, that talk about
politics, and patriotism, and republicanism, and federalism, and Jacksonism, and Hartford Conventionism, and
let any body read in one of 'em half an hour, and his
eyes will be so full of smoke he can't see better than an
owl in the sunshine; he would't be able to tell the
difference between a corn-stalk and the biggest oak tree
in our pasture.

You know, uncle, these Legislaters have had some
dreadful quarrels this winter about a book they call the
constitution: and had to get the Judges of the great
Court to read it to 'em. They made such a fuss about it
I thought it must be a mighty great book, as big agin
as grandfather's great bible. But one day I see one of
the Sinneters have one, and my stars, it was n't so big
as my old spelling book. Thinks I to myself, if ax
handles will buy one, I'll have one and see if I cant read
it myself. So I went into a store where they had a nation sight of books, and asked 'em for a constitution.
They showed me some nice little ones, that they asked
a quarter of a dollar a piece for. I was out of money,
so I told the mon I'd give him four good white oak ax
handles, well finished, for one: and he said, being 'twas
me, I might have it. So now I've got a constitution of
my own, and if I find I can read it, I shall let you
know something about what's in it before a great while.

Your neffu, JACK DOWNING.

LETTER XIV.

Mr. Downing informs his Uncle Joshua that he has a prospect of being nominated for Governor.

To Uncle Joshua Downing up in Downingville.

Portland, April 14, 1830.

UNCLE JOSHUA,—I spose you remember that are story about the two dogs, that uncle Joe Downing used to tell ; how they got to fighting, and snapped and bit, *till they eat each other up, all but jest the tip ends of their tails.* Now I never could exactly see through that story, enough to know how it was done, till lately. I almost thought it was a kind of tough yarn, that had been stretched a good deal. But fact, uncle, I begin to think it's true, every word on't ; for there's something going on here as much like it as two peas in a pod. The Portland Argus and the Portland Advertiser, have fell afowl of each other and gone to biting one another's noses off. And if they keep on as they've began, I guess before summer is out, the'll not only eat each other all up, tails and all, but I believe they are going to devour them are tu outrageous wicked parties, that plagued the legislature so all winter ; I mean the Jacksonites and the Huntonites. They've only been at it a week or two, and they've made quite a hole into 'em aready. The Advertiser eats the Jacksonites, and the Argus eats the Huntonites, and they are thinning of 'em off pretty fast. This will be a great comfort to the State, as it will give the two republican parties a chance to do something another winter. The Advertiser has eat up the Jacksonites in some places away down East, such as Eastport and so on, and away up t'other way in Limerick, and Waterborough, and Fryeburgh.

And the Augus has eaten up the Huntonites in Newfield, and Sanford, and Berwick, and Vinalhaven, and so on. All these towns, on both sides, now have good fair *republican majorities.* I spose about by the middle of next August they 'll get 'em all killed off, so there wont be the skin of a Jacksonite or Huntonite left to be sent to the next legislature.

I hope uncle Joshua, you will be more careful about meddling with politicks ; for so sure as you get hitched on the Jackson party or the Hunton party, these barking, deep-mouthed creatures will fix their teeth upon you, and you'll be munched down before you know it.

There's one thing, uncle, that seems to wear pretty hard upon my mind, and plagues me a good deal ; I havn n't slept but little this tu three nights about it. I wish you would n't say any thing about it up there amongst our folks, for if it should all prove a fudge, they'd be laughing at me. But I tell it to you, because I want your advice, as you've always read the papers, and know considerable about political matters ; tho' to be honest, I don't spose any one knows much more about politics by reading the papers, after all.

But what I was going to tell you, is—now, uncle, don't twist your tobacco chaw over to t'other corner of your mouth and leer over your spectacles, and say Jack's a fool—what I was going to tell you, is this : I see by a paper printed down to Brunswick, that they talk of *nominating me for Governor* to run down Smith and Hunton. Think of that, uncle ; your poor neffu Jack, that last summer was hoeing about among the potatoes, and chopping wood, and making stone walls, like enough before another summer comes about, will be Governor of the State. I shall have a better chance to flog Bill Johnson then, than I should last winter, if we hadn't had no Governor nor no laws ; for I spose a Governor has a right to flog any body he 's a mind to.

But that 's nithers here nor there, uncle ; I want your serious advice. *If they nominate me, had I better accept?* Sometimes I 'm half afraid I should n't understand very well how to du the business ; for I never had a chance to see any governor business done, only what I see Elder Hall du in the Sinnet chamber last winter. Poor man, that makes me think what a time he had going home. I wrote to you before that he went by water, and that the vessel got trig'd by an unconstitutional wind the first day and had to come back again. And he must have found a good many hard trigs after that, for he did n't get home til 2d day of April.

Where he was, in that dreadful storm the 26th of March I have n't heard. But I should think after standing the racket he did last winter in the legislater, and then this ere storm at sea, he never need to fear any thing on land or water again in this world.

I wish you 'd write me what you think about my being a candidate for Governor, and whether you think I could get along with the business. Considerable part of the business I should n't be a mite afraid but what I could du ; that is, *the turning out and putting in.* I know every crook and turn of that business ; for I dont believe there 's a boy in our county, though I say it myself, *that 's turned out and tied up more cattle than I have.* And they say a Governor has a good deal of this sort of work to du.

No more at present from your loving neffu,

JACK DOWNING.

LETTER XV.

Mr. Downing's opinion about Newspapers.

Portland, March 30, 1830.

DEAR UNCLE JACK—In my last letter to Ephraim, I said I should write to you pretty soon something about the Portland Town Meeting. As you've been sleekman and survare a good many years, I suppose you'd like to hear about such kind of things. And I spose I might tell you about a good many other things tu, that you don't have much time to know about away there; and aunt Sally says I ought to; for she says I have a great many advantages living here in Portland, that folks can't have up in the country, and if I should write to some of you once or twice a week, she thinks it would be time well spent. So I shall spend part of my evenings, after I get my day's work done, in writing letters. I don't know but I forgot to tell you that I had hired out here this summer. I get eight dollars a month and board, and have the evenings to myself. I go to school three evenings in a week, and aunt Solly says that she can begin to see that I spell better already. The printer of the Courier and the Family Reader, that sends my letters for me, is very kind; he does'nt ask any thing for sending my letters, and he gives me as many newspapers as I can get time to read. So I spend one evening in the week reading newspapers, and set up pretty late that evening tu. And besides I get a chance to read awhile most every morning before the rest of the folks are up; for these Portland folks are done of your starters in the morning. I've known my father many a time, before the rhumatiz took the poor old gentleman, to mow down an acre of stout grass in the morning, and get done by that time one half the Portland folks leave off snoring. Sometimes I think I better be up in the country tu, mowing or hoeing potatoes, or something else, instead of reading newspapers. Its true they are bewitching kind of things, and like well enough to read 'em, but jest between you and me, they are the worst things to bother a feller's head about that you ever see. In one of my letters you know, I said newspapers were dreadful *smoky* things, and any body couldn't read in 'em half an hour without having their eyes so full of smoke they couldn't tell a pig-sty from a meeting-house.

But I'm thinking after all they are more like *rum* than smoke. You know rum will sometimes set quite

peaceable folks together by the ears, and make them
quarrel like mad dogs—so do the newspapers. Rum
makes folks act very *silly*—so do the newapepers. Rum
makes folks *see double*—so do the newspapers. Sometimes rum gets folks so they can't see at all—so do the
newspapers. Rum, if they take tu much of it, makes
folks *sick to the stomach*—so do the newspapers. Rum
makes folks go rather *crooked*, reeling from one side of
the road to tother—and the newspapers make one half
the politicians *cross their path* as often as any drunkard
you ever see. It was the newspapers, uncle Joshua,
that made you *bet* about the Speaker last summer, and
lose your bushel of corn. Remember that, uncle, and
dont believe any thing you see in the papers this summer, unless you see it in the Daily Courier or Family
Reader ; and dont you believe them neither if ever you
see them smoke like the rest of the papers.

As I was a saying about my evenings, I spend one
evening a week reading that little book called the constitution, that kept our legislators quarrelling all winter. You know I bought one for four ax-handles; I find
I can read it considerable easy, most all of it without
spelling, and when I get through I shall tell you something about it.

A queer thought, uncle, has just popt into my head:
I guess I should make a capital member of Congress—
for this letter is just like one of the Congress speeches.
It begun about the town meeting, but not a bit of a word
is there in it from beginning to end about the town meeting, after you get over the text. But I find by reading
the papers that when a Congress man speaks all day
without touching his subject, he makes a motion to adjourn, and goes at it again the next day. So I believe
I must say good night to you now, and try it again the
next leisure evening.

Your loving neffu,

JACK DOWNING.

LETERR XVI.

The distinction between political parties described.

Portland, June 9, 1830.

UNCLE JOSHUA,—Did you ever see tu dogs get to quarrelling about one bone? How they will snap and snarl about it, especially if they are hungry. Sometimes one will get it into his mouth and took it away like smoke, and t'other arter him full chisel. And when he overtakes him they'll have another scratch, and drop the bone, and then t'other one 'll get it, and off he goes like a shot. And sometimes they both get hold together, one at one end and one at t'other, and then sich a tugging and growlin you never see. Well now, when they act so, they act just like the Portland Argus and Portland Advertiser; two great big growlers, they are all the time quarrelling about their *Republikin,* to see which will have it. If the Advertiser says any thing about his republikin, the Argus snaps at it, and says 'tis n't your republikin, its mine. You no business to be a republikin, you are a Federalist.

And when the Argus says any thing about his republikin, the Advertiser flies up, and says, you no business to be a republikin, you're a Jacksonite. And so they have it up hill and down, bark, bark, and tug, tug, and which 'll get the republikin at last I cant tell. Sometimes they get so mad, seems as though they'll tear each other all to pieces, and there's forty thousand folks setting of 'em on and hollering stooboy. Now there was n't any need of all this quarrel, for each of 'em had a republikin last winter; the Argus had a democratic one, and the Advertiser had a national one, and they got 'em mixed by leaving off the *chrissen names.* And I guess it would puzzle a Philadelphy lawyer to tell 'em apart without their names, for their republikins are as much alike as tu peas in a pod.

The Advertiser never should say *republikin* alone, but *national* republikin, and the Argus never should

D

say republikin alone, but *democratic* republican. And
then it seems as though each one might know his own
bone, and knaw it without quarrelling.

I thought, uncle, I'd jest tell you a little about this
ere business, because I know you always want to find
out all the kinks about politiks.

Your neffu,

JACK DOWNING.

P. S. I dont hear any thing yet about the convention up there that you promised to make to nominate
me for Governor. I think it is time it was out , for I
am afraid Mr. Hunton and Mr. Smith will get the start
of me, if I aint under way soon.

J. D.

LETTER XVII.

Proceedings of the Great Caucus at Downingville.

From the Portland Courier of July 21, 1830.

☞ **THE LONG AGONY OVER,** ☜

And my Nomination out.

We delay this paper something beyond the usual hour
of publication in order to lay before our readers the important intelligence received yesterday from Downingville.—This we have been able to accomplish, tho' not
without extraordinary exertions and extra help. But
the crisis is important, we had almost said appalling,
and demands of every patriotic citizen of Maine the
highest sacrifices in his power to make. The important
proceedings of the grand convention at Downingville
reached here, by express, yesterday about a quarter before 3 o'clock, P. M. having travelled the whole distance
notwithstanding the extreme high temperature of the
weather, at the rate of thirteen and a half miles an hour.

And but for an unfortunate occurrence, it would undoubtedly have reached here at least three hours earlier *Capt. Jehu Downing*, who with his characteristic magnanimity and patriotism volunteered to bring the express the whole way, having taken a high spirited steed for the first ten miles, was unfortunately thrown to the ground in attempting to leap a barrier which lay across the road. Two of his ribs were broken by the fall, and his right arm so badly fractured that it is feared amputation must be resorted to, besides several other severe contusions on various parts of the body. We are happy to hear however that Doctor Zachariah Downing, who on hearing the melancholy intelligence very promptly repaired to the spot to offer his professional services, pronounces the Captain out of danger, and also that the Captain bears his misfortune with his accustomed fortitude, expressly declaring that the only regret he feels on the occasion is the delay of the express. Here is patriotism, a devotedness to the welfare of the country, and to genuine democratic republican principles, worthy of the days of the revolution.

Lieut. Timothy Downing forwarded the express the remainder of the way with the utmost despatch, having run down three horses, one of which died on the road. —But we keep our readers too long from the gratifying intelligence received.

Great Democratic National Republican Convention.

Downingville, Monday, July 19, 1830.

At a large and respectable meeting of the democratic national republicans of Downingville and the neighboring parts of the state, convened this day at the centre school house, the meeting was called to order by the venerable and silver-haired patriarch, old Mr. *Zebedee Downing*, who had not been out to a political meeting before for the last twenty-five years. The venerable old gentleman stated in a few feeling remarks the object of the meeting; that he had not meddled with politics since the days of Jefferson: but that know in view of the awful calamities which threatened to involve our country in total ruin, he felt it his duty the little remaining time he might be spared from the grave, to lift up his voice and his example before his children, grand children, and great grand children whom he saw gathered around him, and encourage them to save the country for which he had fought and bled in his younger years. After the enthusiastic applause elicited by these remarks, the old gentleman called for the nomination of a chairman, and JOSHUA DOWNING, ESQUIRE was unanimously called to the chair, and Mr. *Ephraim Downing* appointed Secretary.

On motion of Mr. Jacob Downing, voted, that a committee of five be appointed to draft resolutions to lay before this meeting. Whereupon, Jotham Downing. Ichabob Downing, Zenas Downing, Levi Downing, and Isaiah Downing, were appointed said committee, and after retiring about five minutes they returned and reported the following preamble and resolutions.

Whereas an awful crisis has arrived in the political affairs of our country, our public men all having turned traitors, and resolved to ruin the country, and make us and our children all slaves forever; and whereas our ship of state and our ship of the United States, are both driven with tremendous violence before the fury of the political tempest, and are just upon the point of being dashed upon the breakers of political destruction; and whereas, nothing short of the most prompt and vigorous exertions of the patriotic democratic national republicans of this state and of the United States can avert the impending danger.

And whereas, the Jacksonites, and Adamsites, and Huntonites, and Smithites, have so multiplied in the land, and brought things to such a pass, that our liberties are unquestionably about to receive their doom forever:

Therefore Resolved, that it is the highest and most

sacred duty of every patriotic Democratic National Republican in the State, to arouse himself and buckle on his political armour, and make one last, one mighty effort to save the state and the country, and place the constitution once more upon a safe and firm foundation.

Resolved, that the awful crisis of affairs in this State requires a firm devoted patriot, a high-minded and gifted statesman, and a uniform unwavering Democratic National Republican, for chief magistrate.

Resolved, that in this awful crisis, we believe the eyes of all true patriots are turned upon

THE HON. JACK DOWNING,

late of Downingville. but since last winter a resident in Portland, the capital of the State.

Resolved, that we have the fullest confidence in the talents, integrity, moral worth, tried patriotism, and unwavering and unchangeable sterling Democratic National Republicanism of the *Hon. Jack Downing*, and that his election to the office of Governor in September next, and nothing else, can save the State from total, unutterable, and irretrievable ruin.

Resolved therefore, that we recommed him to the electors of this State as a candidate for said office, and that we will use all fair and honourable means, and, if necessary, will not stick at some a little *dis*-honourable, to secure his election.

Resolved, that we disapprove of personal crimination and re-crimination in political contests, and therefore will only say of our opponents, that we think them no better than they should be, and that they unquestionably mean to destroy the land we live in.

Resolved, that it be recommended to all the patriotic democratic national republicans throughout the State, to be up and doing; to call county meetings, town meetings, school district meetings, and village and bar-room meetings, and proceed to organise the party as fast as possible, by appointing standing committees, and central committees, and corresponding committees, and bearers and distributors of handbills; and in short by doing every thing that the good of the cause and the salvation of the country requires.

Resolved, conditionally, that in case General Jackson should be likely to be re-elected, we highly and cordially approve of his administration, and believe him to be second to none but Washington; but in case he should stand no chance of re-election, we resolve him to be the ignorant tool of a corrupt faction, plotting to destroy the liberties of the country.

Resolved, that the thanks of this convention be presented to Miss Abigail Downing, for the use of her school room this afternoon, she having with a generous patriotism dismissed her school for that purpose.

Resolved, that the proceedings of this convention, signed by the chairman and secretary, be published in the *Portland Daily Courier*, and the *Family Reeder*, the official organs of the Hon. JACK DOWNING's correspondence, and any other genuine Democratic National Republican papers in the State.

JOSHUA DOWNING, CHAIRMAN.

Attest: EPHRAIM DOWNING, *Secretary.*

We are assured by Lieutenant Timothy Downing, with whom we had a short interview, that the best spirit prevailed in the convention; not a dissenting voice was heard, and all the resolutions passed unanimously. We add an extract or two from private letters.

From Ephraim Downing, to the Hon. Jack Downing.

" Well, Jack, if you don't acknowledge we've done the thing up in style, you're no gentleman and not fit for Governor. I wish you to be very particular to keep the Sheriff's office for me.—Father says cousin Jeremiah has thrown out some hints that he shall have the Sheriff's office. But butter my ristbands, if you do give it to

him you'll go out of office again next year, that's posi-
tive. Jere's a clear factionist, you may rely upon that.
No, no, stick to your old friends, and they'll stick to
you. I'm going to start to-morrow morning on an elec-
tioneering cruise. I shall drum 'em up about right.
You only keep a stiff upper lip, and you'll come in all
hollow. "

From Joshua Downing, Esq. to the Hon. Jack Downing.

" Dear Jack, things look well here; with proper exertions I think you may rely upon suceess. I am in great
haste, and write this jest to tell you to be sure and not
promise a single office to any mortal living, till I see you.
These things must be managed very prudently, and you
will stand in need of the counsel of your old uncle. I
think I could do as much good to the state by being appointed Land Agent, as any way; but I'll determine
upon that when I see you.

N. B. Make no promises.

Your affectionate uncle,

JOSHUA.

LETTER XVIII.

Particulars and Returns of the Caucus.

To the Hon. Jack Downing, Portland.

Downingville, Monday Eve, September 13, 1860.

DEAR JACK,—I have just returned, puffing and blowing, from town-meeting, and have only time to tell you
that we gave you a confounded good run here. If your
friends in the rest of the State have done their duty, you
are elected by an overwhelming majority. The vote in
this town for governor stood as follows:—

Hon. Jack Downing,	87
Hon. Samuel E. Smith,	00
Hon. Jonathan G. Hunton,	00

Capt. Jehu Downing is elected representative; it was thought to be due to him by the party for his magnanimous exertions in carrying the express to Portland at the time you were nominated by our grand convention.

In great haste, your uncle,

JOSHUA DOWNING.

LETTER XIX.

Mr. Downing's ingenious scheme to get an office.

Portland, Dec. 13, 1830.

DEAR UNCLE JOSHUA:—I am tired of hard work, and I mean to have an office some how or other yet. Its true I and all our family got rather dished in the governor business; if I'd only got in, they should every soul of 'em had an office. down to the forty-ninth cousin. But its no use to cry for spilt milk. I've got another plan in my head; I find the United States offices are the things to make money in, and if I can get hold of a good fat one, you may appoint a day of thanksgiving up there in Downingville, and throw by your work every one of you as long as you live.

I want you to set me up for member of Congress up there, and get me elected as soon as you can, for if I can get on to Washington I believe I can work it so as to get an office somehow or other.—I want you to be particular to put me up as a Tariff man. I was agoing to take sides against the tariff so as to please Gineral Jackson and all his party, for they deal out the offices now a days, and you know they've been mad enough

with the tariff to eat it up. But the Portland Advertiser has been blowin away lately and praising up the
tariff and telling what a fine thing tis, and fact, *it has
brought the old gineral round.* His great long message
to Congress has just got along here, and the old gentleman says the tariff wants a little mendin, but on the
whole it's a cute good thing, and we must n't give it up.

Your lovin neffu,
JACK DOWNING.

LETTER XX.

*Cousin Nabby describes the Temperance of Downing-
ville.*

Downingville, Jinerwary, 20, 1831.

To Cousin Sarah Downing, at School down to Portland.

I should like to know, cousin Sarah, if you have heard
down there to Portland any thing about a *temperance society.* If you have just write and tell me what it means.
You know father wants to know the meaning of every
thing, and so I walked tu miles over to the school-master's
to borry Mr. Walker's dictionary to see what it meant;
and after all I want no wiser than I was afore, for there
wasn't one word in it about temperance societies. Tother
day father sot in the shop door, wondering if Jack would
go to the Congress or not, when a proper great fat red-
faced man came in, and opened a long paper with more
names on it than I could read in a week,—and says he,
Mr. Downing, I want you to sine your name to this paper.
Father took hold of the paper with one hand, and run
tother up under his hat, jest as he always does when he
tries to think; and, my friend, says he, I dont know as I
quite understand what this ere means. Why, says he,

by putting your name down, you promise not to drink
any rum yourself, nor to let any of your family. My conscience, father understood it then, I can tell you, he
hopped rite out of his chair, and I guess the temperance
man was gone in no time. Well, after father had time
to consider a little he began to feel afraid he had n't
used the man exactly right; for, said he, may be all
places aint like Downingville. I remember reading in
the newspaper of some places where they drink rum as
we do water, and get so drunk that they tumble about
on the ground. And may be the man did n't know but
what we drank it here. And if he was trying to do good
he was n't so much to blame after all. Indeed, Sam,
said he, for Mr. Josslyn came in while he was talking,
I've been told there are shop keepers who retale rum by
the half jill, to men who drink it at their counters, and
some can actually bare that enormous quantity two and
three times in a day. I never see Sam's eyes so big,
Sarah; he look'd as if he wanted to say, that's a whack-
er, Mr. Downing; and so thinks I, I will write to Sarah,
and she 'll tell me all about it.

Your loving cousin,   NABBY.

P. S. I tried to tell what father said in his own words,
cause you always like to hear him talk. Sam says
Sarah dont understand such things; the libry is only fit
for folks like her and the schoolmaster. A farmer ort
to stick to his ox bows and goard sticks. And I believe
he's half rite, Sarah, for I dont believe you are so happy
for trying to no so much; ever since you took to study,
I see you dont laugh half so hearty as you used to, and
you look sober three times as often. I 'm afraid you
will be a spoilt girl for the country, Sarah; you 'd better
leave your hard words and come up here and sing at
your wheel all day, churn butter and milk the cows, go
to slay rides and quiltings, and be as good and happy
as you used to be. I love you, Sarah, and always shall,
and I believe Sam would like you as well as he duz me,
if twant for your learnin. There, I wont say another
word, for I'm half cryin now.   N.

LETTER XXI.

*Mr. Downing's account of the dreadful tussle in which
the Jacksonites in the legislature attempt to pour a
" healing act" down the Huntonite's throats.*

Portland, Feb. 4, 1831.

DEAR UNCLE JOSHUA.—If you got my postscript to
this letter that I sent you yesterday, I spose you wont
sleep nor eat much till you hear something more about
it. So I thought I'd try to send you a little bit of a letter to-day. O dear, uncle, there 's terrible times here
again, and I'm half afraid it's agoing to be worse than
it was last winter. The Legislater 's been all in the
wind this two or three days, pulling and hauling and
fighting like smoke. The wheels of governments are all
stopt ; I can say as they are *trigged,* as they used to be
last winter, but they are fairly stopped, because nobody
dont pull 'em along ; for when the members are all pulling each other's caps, how can they pull the wheels of
government ? They seemed to get along very well ever
since they've been here till now, and I thought they most
all belonged to them are two clever parties that tried so
hard to save the State last winter ; I mean the democratic republicans and the national republicans. But
some how or other this week a quarrelsome gang of
Jacksonites and Huntonites has got into the Legislater
and kicked up such a bobbery, it seems as though they'd
tare the State all to pieces. My heart 's been up in my
mouth a dozen times for fear the State would go to ruin
before I could get out of it ; and I've scratched round
and picked up what few bean-poles and ax-handles I
had left, and got all ready to sail to Boston, for I'me
determined to be off before the State goes to rack. And
I advise you and all our friends at Downingville to pack
up as soon as you get this letter, and be all ready as
soon as you hear a cracking down this way to fly for
your lives away back into New-Hampshire or Vermont.

The trouble as near as I could understand it begun in this way. The Jacksonites said the Huntonites worked so hard last winter in trying to trig the wheels of government, and tare the constitution to pieces, that they made themselves all sick, dreadful sick, and had n't got well yet; and it was time to do something to try to cure 'em ; for their sickness was so catching that all the State would be taken down with it in a little while, if they want cured.

But the Huntonites said they want sick a bit; they never was better in their lives ; and moreover, it was false that they had tried to trig the wheels of government last winter, or tear a single leaf out of the constitution ; if any thing of that kind was done, they said the Jacksonites did it, and as for taking doctor's stuff they'd no notion of it. But the Jacksonites said 'twas no use, the Huntonites were all sick, and they must take some doctor stuff, and if they would n't take it willingly they must be *made* to take it. So they went to work and fixed a dose that they called a *healing act*, that they said would cure all the Huntonites and any body else that had catched the sickness of 'em. The Huntonites declared 'twas no use for 'em to fix it, they never would take it as long as they lived, that's what they wouldn't; they were as well as any body, and they'd fight it out till next June before they'd take it. Howsomever, the Jacksonites got their dose ready, and yesterday they carried it into the House of Representatives and told the Huntonites they must take it, and 'twould do 'em good. As soon as the Huntonites smelt of it, they turned up their noses, and said no, before they'd take that are plaguy dirty stuff they'd fight 'em all over the State, inch by inch. But the Jacksonites said 'twas no use, they might sniff as much as they pleased, it was the only thing that would cure 'em, and they must take it, and more than all that, they was the strongest and they *should* take it.

Some of the Huntonites looked pale as tho' they were a little grain frightened, and some of them looked red as though they were mad as a March hair. And some of 'em begun to talk to the Jacksonites and tell 'em how unreasonable it was to make 'em take doctor stuff when they want sick. They were well now, and like as not if they should take it, 'twould make 'em all sick.

One of 'em, that talked like a very clever man got up and coaxed 'em to ask the Judges of the great Court if they thought there was any *need* of their taking sich a dose, or if it would do 'em any good if they did take it. But the Jacksonites said no, they shouldn't ask no sich questions. They understood the business well enough, they knew the Huntonites were sick, and they knew this would cure 'em, and swallow it they should. Well, the Huntonites see how 'twas gone goose with 'em, and they thought the only chance left was to put their hands over their mouths and fight and kick and scrabble with all their might and keep it out of their throats as long as they could. Still they tried to talk and reason with the Jacksonites about it. They asked 'em to let them have time to examine the medicine carefully and see what it was made of, or that they would tell 'em what it was made of, or why they thought it would do any good to take it. But the Jacksonites said they should n't tell 'em any thing about it, it would be ' casting pearls before swine,' and the good book said they must n't do so.

The men who had fixed the dose knew what they were about, they had fixed it right, and the Huntonites must open their mouths and take it, and not parley any more about it. And now the rale tussle and the hard fight begun. The House seemed to be so full of Jacksonites and Huntonites that I guess there was n't but a few republicans left. And I could n't help minding that the Jacksonites took the seats of the democratic republicans, and the Huntonites took the seats of the national republicans. Well, the Jacksonites took the dose in one hand, and grab'd the Huntonites with the other, and tipped their heads back, and were jest agoing to pour it down their throats, when the Huntonites

E

fetched a spring and kicked it away to the fourth day of April. But the Jacksonites run after it and got it back again in about half an hour, and clinched 'em again, and got all ready to pour it down ; but jest as they got it almost to their lips, the Huntonites fetched another spring and kicked it away to the fourth of March. Away went the Jacksonites after it again, and brought it back, and clinched the Huntonites in the same manner as before, and they kicked it away again, but they didn't kick this time quite to the end of February.

So they kept it agoing all the forenoon, but every time the Huntonites kick'd the bitter dose away, it didn't go so far as it did the last time before. I spose they begun to grow tired and could n't kick so hard. Well, then they tried to adjourn so as to get some dinner, but the Jacksonites would n't let 'em, And they kept 'em there till four o'clock in the afternoon without any dinner, and I dont know but they thought the Huntonites would get so hungry after a while that they would swallow it down without much fuss. But it all would n't do, the nearer it come to 'em, the tighter the Huntonites gritted their teeth together, and I guess they'd a starved before they would take it. Well after the Jacksonites had tried nearly twenty times to pour down the bitter dose, and the Huntonites had kicked it away as many times, both parties seemed to be nearly tired out, and so they finally agreed to adjourn till nine o'clock this morning. I thought the Huntonites, if they once got out, would cut and run home and get clear of the plaguy stuff. But instead of that they all come in again this morning, and they've been at it again all day, hammer and tongs, the Jacksonites trying to pour it down, and the Huntonites fighting against it, tooth and nail.

How it 'll come out I cant tell. Whether the State will be ruined if they dont take it, I cant tell ; or whether it will cure them if they do take it, I can't tell. But I can assure you, dear uncle, there's a greater fuss here, than there was when the little boy said he run and jumped over a fence and tore his trowses as if the heavens and earth were coming to pieces. If we live through it, I shall let you know something more about it.

Your lovin neffu,

JACK DOWNING.

LETTER XXII.

An account of the manner in which the "healing act" was crammed down the Huntonites' throats.

Portland, Saturday, March 5, 1831.

DEAR UNCLE JOSHUA,—I aint dead, but I spose you begin to feel kind of uneasy about me, bein I have n't writ home so long. Well, I'll tell you 'twas; I've had *this ere cold* and one thing or another, so bad, I did n't feel hardly smart enough to write. And besides I got so skeer'd that night the Jacksonites poured their doctor stuff, what they call the healing plaster down the throates of the Huntonites, that I did n't dare to go nigh 'em again for a good while for fear they'd pour some of their pesky stuff down my throat. But I'am sorry I did n't write afore, for I've let it alone so long now, that my work has got desputly behindhand. When I writ to you before, the Jacksonites were holding the Huntonites by the hair of the head with one hand and trying to cram the healing plaster down their throats with 'tother, and the Huntonites were kicking and scrambling, and gritting their teeth together with all their might, and doubling up their fists and stamping, and declaring up hill and down, that they would never take it. And they were so obstropulous about it for a while. I did n't know as they ever would swallow it. But the Jacksonites were the stoutest, and held on to 'em like a dog to a root, and kept 'em there all the day and all the evening till about midnight, and then the poor Huntonites seemed to be a most dragged out. I fairly pitied 'em. Along in the first of it they threatened pretty stoutly, and declared by every thing that's black and blue, if they had to take this dirty dose and should happen to be strongest next year, they'd make the Jacksonites take a dose worth two of this. But all the threatening did n't do any good; and then they fell to begging and coaxing, and that did n't do any good nother. The Jacksonites said they should not only take it, but they should take it that night before they slept. At last they got their hands and feet tied, and kept bringin it up a little nearer and little nearer to their mouths, and the Huntonites got so they could n't do nothing but *spit*. But the Jacksonites did n't mind the spitting, for you know it is n't for the doctor to stand about being spit upon a little, when he's giving medicine. Just before the last ont, the poor Huntonites rolled their eyes dreadfully, and I believe some on 'em lost their senses a little; one of 'em took a notion that they were going to make him swallow a whole live goose, feathers and all, and he begged of 'em, if they would n't take out the gizzard and t'other inside things, that they'd jest pull out the pin feathers, so that it would n't scratch his throat going down. But they did n't pay no attention to him, and just before the clock struck twelve they grabbed 'em by the throat, and pried their mouths open, and poured it in. The Huntonites guggled a little, but they had to swallow it. A day or two afterwards they made some of the Sinneters take it in the same way. They had a considerable tussle for it, but not quite so bad as they had in the House.

Some thought this healing dose would make the Huntonites worse, and some thought it would make 'em better. I've watch'd 'em ever since they took it whenever I dared to go near the Legislater, and I can't see much alteration in 'm. But that, or something else, has kicked up a monstrous dust amongst other folks all over the world amost. I've been looking over the newspapers a little, and I never see the world in such a terrible hubbub before in all my life. Every body seems to be running mad, and jest ready to eat each other up. There's Russia snapping her teeth like a great bear, and is just agoing to eat up the Poles, I don't mean Ephraim's bean poles, but all the folks that live in Poland; not that are Poland up there where Mr. Dunn lives, but that great Poland over alongside of Russia. And there's the Dutch trying to eat up Holland, and the Belgians are trying to eat up the Dutch, and ther's 'five great powers' trying to pour a healing dose down the throat of the king of the Netherlands, and there's Mr. O'Connell trying to make the king of England and Parliament take a healing dose, and there's Ireland jest ready to eat up Mr. O'Connell, and all the kings of Europe are trying to eat up the people, and the people are all trying to eat up the kings.

And our great folks in this country too, away off there to Washington, have got into such a snarl, I guess it would puzzle a Philadelphy lawyer to get 'em out of it. There's the President and Mr. Calhoun and Mr. Van Buren and the two great republican papers, and half a dozen more of 'em, all together by the ears; but which of 'em will eat up the rest I don't know. I have heard a good many guess that Mr. Van Buren would eat up the whole toat of 'em; for they say although he is a small man, there isn't another man in the country, that can eat his way through a political pudding so slick as he can. These are dreadful times, uncle; I don't know what 'll become of the world, if I dont get an office pretty soon.

It seems to me there must be something out of the way to make so much confusion in the world; and I hope the Legislater before they adjourn will pass a general healing act to cure all these difficulties. They 've been talking about passing a healing act to cure our State House up to Augusta, for they say its two small, and they intend to bring it down here to Portland to cure it. But I guess it 'll give 'em a pull, for they say the Kennebeckers are master fellers to hold on.

E 2

They had a kind of flusteration here to-day in the Legislater. The Speaker 's cleared out, and left 'em, because the Governor said he'd taken his turn sitting in the *Chair* long enough, and he must go and sit on the *Bench* awhile now. And then they went to work and chose that good natured man from Monmouth for Speaker. I meant to a told you about them are two great meetings they 've had here to make Governors and Presidents and one thing another: but I haven't time to-day.

One of 'm made Mr. Smith Governor for next year and Gineral Jackson President; and t'other made Mr. Sprague governor, and kind of put Mr. Clay a brewing for President.

If you think its best for me to run again for governor another year I wish you'd call our friends together up there and have me nominated, for there's nothing like starting in season in these matters.

Your loving neffu,
JACK DOWNING.

LETTER XXIII.

Mr. Downing's Poetical dream.

Portland, Saturday, April 2, 1831.

Dear Cousin Nabby,—I dont hardly know whether to send this letter to you, or uncle Joshua. You know I always send all the the politics and Legislaters to uncle; but this ere one's most all poetry, and they say that stuff belongs to the ladies. So I believe on the whole I shall send it to you. Dont you be skeer'd now because I 've made some poetry, for I dont think it 'll hurt me; I dont feel crazy for nothing. But I'll just tell you how it happened. Last night I was in the Le-

gislater and they sot out to make a law to tax old bachelors. They tried pretty hard to make it, and I
thought one spell they 'd get it. I felt kind of bad about
it because I knew it would bear so hard upon cousin
Obediah. Well, I went home and went to bed, and I
dont know what the matter was, but I had a kind of a
queer night of it; and when I got up in the morning
there was a soft sort of sickish stuff kept running off
of my tongue, jest like a stream of chalk. Pray tell
me what you think of it: here it is.

I dreamed a dream in the midst of my slumbers,
And, as fast as I dream'd, it was coined into numbers,
My thoughts ran along in such beautiful metre,
I'am sure I ne'er saw any poetry sweeter.
It seem'd that a law had been recently made,
That a tax on old bachelors' pates should be laid.
And in order to make them all willing to marry,
The tax was as large as a man could well carry.
The Bachelors grumbled, and said 't were no use,
'T was cruel injustice and horrid abuse,
And declar'd that to save their own heart's blood from spilling,
Of such a vile tax they would ne'er pay a shilling.
But the Rulers determined their scheme to pursue,
So they set all the bachelors up at vendue.
A crier was sent thro' the town to and fro,
To rattle his bell, and his trumpet to blow,
And to bawl out at all he might meet in the way,
" Ho ! forty old bachelors sold here to day,"
And presently all the old maids in the town,
Each one in her very best bonnet and gown,
From thirty to sixty, fair, plain, red and pale,
Of every description, all flocked to the sale.
The auctioneer then in his labors began,
And called out aloud, as he held up a man,
" How much for a bachelor ? who wants to buy ?"
In a twink every maiden responded—" I—I."

In short, at a hugely extravagant price,
The bachelors all were sold off in a trice;
And forty old maidens, some younger, some older,
Each lugged an old bachelor home on her shoulder.

JACK DOWNING.

LETTER XXIV.

*The blow up of President Jackson's first Cabinet puts
a new kink into Mr. Downing's head, and the result.*

Portland, April 26, 1831.

DEAR UNCLE JOSHUA,—I'm in considerable of a
kind of a flusteration to-day, because I've got a new
sceme in my head. New ideas, you know, are always
apt to give me the agitations a little; so you mustn't
wonder if my letter this time does have some rather
odd things in it. I don't know when I've had such a
great scheme in my head afore. But you know I was
always determined to make something in the world,
and if my friends 'll only jest stick by me, I shall make
common folks stare yet. Some thought it was a pretty
bold push my trying to get in to be governor last year;
and some have laughed at me, and said I come out at
the little end of the horn about it, and that I'd better
staid up to Downingville and hoed potatoes, than to be
fishing about for an office and not get any more votes
than I did. But they can't see through a millstone so
fur as I can. Altho' I didn't get in to be governor, its
made me known in the world, and made considerable
of a great man of me, so that I shall stand a much better chance to get an office if I try again. But I must
make haste and tell you what I am at, for I am in a
great hurry. I guess you'll stare when I tell you the
next letter you'll get from me will be dated at Wash-

ington, or else somewhere on the road between here and there.

O, uncle, we have had some great news here from Washington ; every body's up in arms about it, and can't hardly tell what to think of it. They say the President's four great Secretaries have all resigned ; only think of that, uncle. And they say their salaries were *six thousand dollars a-year;* only jest think of that, uncle. Six thousand dollars a year. Why, a governor's salary is a fool to it. On the whole, I'm glad I didn't get the governor's office. I shall start for Washington to-morrow morning ; or I don't know but I shall start to-night, if I can get ready, and travel all night. Its best to be in season in such things, and I shall have to go rather slow, for I've got pretty considerable short of money, and expect I shall have to foot it part way. I shall get there in about a fortnight, and I'm in hopes to be in season to get one of them are offices. I think it's the duty of all true republicans that have the good of the country at heart, to take hold and help the President along in these trying difficulties.— For my part, I am perfectly willing to take one of the offices, and I hope some other good men will come right forward and take the others. What a shame 'twas that them are Secretaries should all clear out, and leave the poor old General to do all the work alone. Why, uncle, they'd no more patriotism than your old hoss.

But I must n't stop to parley about it now; what I want to say is, I wish you to write a recommendation to the President for me to have one of his offices, and go round as quick as you can and get all our friends at Downingville to sign it, and send it on to Washington as fast as possible; for it would be no more than right that I should show the President some kind of recommendation before he gives me the office. I want you to tell the President that I've always been one of his strongest friends; and you know I always have spoke well of him, and *in fact he is the best President we ever had.* It might be well for you to quote this last sentence as an ' extract from a letter of the Hon. Jack Downing.' It would give the President some confidence in my friendship, and the ' Hon.' would convince him that I am a man of some standing in the State.

Now you keep up a good heart, uncle ; you have always had to delve hard all your days up there on the old farm, and you've done considerable to boost me up into an office, and if I get hold of these six thouand dollars a year, you shall have a slice out of it that will make your old heels felt light again.   I haven't named it to a single soul here except cousin Sally, and I want it to be kept a profound secret till I get the office, so as to make them are chaps that have been a sneering at me here, stare like an owl in a thunder shower.   And, besides, if it should leak out that I was going, I'm afraid somebody else might get the start of me, for there are always enough that have their mouth open when it rains such rich porrage.   But it's like as not, the newspapers 'll blab it out before I get half way there.   And you needn't think strange, if you see some of the Boston or New York papers in a few days saying, 'The Hon. Jack Downing passed through this city yesterday, on his way to Washington.   It is rumoured, that he is to be called upon to fill one of the vacant offices.'— But I must stop, for it is time I was picking up my duds for a start.   Sally has been darning my stockings all the morning.   Love to Aunt and Cousin Nabby, and all of 'em.   Good by.

Your loving neffu,

JACK DOWNING.

LETTER XXV.

Mr. Downing on his way to assist Jackson, at Washington, stops at Boston—his conversation with the Boston Editors.

City of New York, May 4, 1831.

DEAR UNCLE JOSHUA,—I have got so fur at last, and a pretty hard run I've had of it to get here, I can tell ye. This running after offices is pretty tuff work for poor folks. Sometimes I think there aint much profit in it after all, any more than there is in buying lottery tickets, where you pay a dollar and sometimes get four shillings back, and sometimes nothing. Howsomever I dont mean to be discouraged yet, for if I should give out now and go back again, them are sassy chaps in Portland would laff at me worse than they did afore.— What makes me feel kind of down hearted about it, is because I've seen in the newspapers that tu of them are good offices at Washington are gone aready. One Mr. Livingston 's got one of 'em, and Mr. Woodbury that lives up in New Hampshire 's got tother, and I'm considerable afraid the others will be gone before I get there.

I want you to be sure and get my recommendation into the post office as soon as you can, so it may get there as soon as I do. It's a week to-day since I started from Portland, and if I have good luck I'm in hopes to get there in about a week more. Any how, I shall worry along as fast as I can. I have to foot it more than three-quarters of the way, because the stage folks ask so much to ride, and my money's pretty near gone. But if I can only jest get there before the offices are gone I think I shall get one of 'em, for I got a good string of recommendations in Boston as I come along. I never thought of getting any recommendations of strangers, till a man I was travelling with, kind of talked round and round, and found out what I was after.

And then says he, if you want to make out, you must get the newspaper folks to give you a lift, for they manage these matters. And he told me I better get some of the Boston Editors to recommend me, or it would be no use for me to go.

I thought the man was more than half right, so when I got into Boston I called round to see the editors.— They all seemed very glad to see me, when I told 'em who I was; and I never see a better set of true republicans any where in the State of Maine. And when I told 'em that I was always a true republican, and my father and grand father were republicans before me, they all talked so cleaver about patriotism, and our republican institutions, and the good of the people, that I could n't help thinking it was a plaguy shame there should be any such wicked parties as Federalists, or Huntonites, or Jacksonites, to try to tare the country to pieces and plague the republicans so.

This dont include President Jackson. He is n't a Jacksonite, you know; he's a true republican as there is in Downingville. I had a talk with the Boston Patriot man first. He said he would give me a recommendation with a good deal of pleasure; and when I got my office at Washington I must stick to the good old republican cause like wax; and if all true republicans were only faithful to the country, Henry Clay, the republican candidate, will come in all hollow.

He'll be next President, says he, jest as sure as your name is Jack Downing. Then I went to see the editor of the Boston Gazette. He said he certainly should be very happy to give me a recommendation; and he trusted when I got to Washington where I should have considerable influence, I should look well to the interests of the republican party. He said there was an immense sight of intrigue and underhand work going on by the enemies of the country to ruin Mr. Calhoun, the republican candidate for President. But he said they would'nt make out; Mr. Calhoun had found out their tricks, and the republicans of old Virginny and

South Carolina were all up in arms about it, and if we republicans of the northern states would only take hold and fight for the good cause, Mr. Calhoun would be elected as true as the sun will rise to-morrow.

The next I went to see was the editor of the Boston Statesman. He seemed to be a little shy of me at first, and was afraid I want a true republican; and wanted to know if I did n't run against Governor Smith last year down there in Maine. I told him I had seen Governor Smith a number of times in Portland, but I was sure I never run against him in my life, and did n't think I ever came within a rod of him. Well he wanted to know if I was n't a candidate for Governor in opposition to Mr. Smith. I told him no, I was a candidate on the same side. Was n't you, said he, looking mighty sharp at me, *was 'nt you one of the federal candidates for governor?* My stars, uncle Joshua, I never felt my hair curl quicker than it did then. My hand kind of draw'd back and my fingers clinched as if I was jest agoing to up fist and knock him down To think that he should charge me with being a *federal candidate* it was too much for flesh and blood to bear. But I cooled down as quick as I could, for fear it might hurt me about getting my office. I told him I never was a federal candidate, and there never was a drop of federal blood in me; and I would run from a federalist if I should meet one as quick as I would from *poison.* That's right, says he, I like that, that's good stuff, and he catched hold of my hand and give it such a shake, I did n't know but he'd a pull'd it off.

He said he would give me the best recommendation he could write, and when I got to Washington I must stick to the old Gineral like the tooth ach, for the federalists were intriguing dreadfully to root him out of his office and upset the republican party. If the republicans could only be kept together, he said President Jackson, the republican candidate, could be elected as easy as a cat could lick her ear; but if we suffered ourselves to be divided it would be gone goose with us, and

F

the country would be ruined. So you must stick to the
re-election of Gineral Jackson, said he, *at all events;* and
then he kind of whispered in my ear, and says he, in
case any thing should happen, if Gineral Jackson should
be sick or any thing, you must remember that Mr. Van
Buren is the *republican candidate.*

I told him he never need to fear me; I should stick
to the republican party thro' thick and thin. So I took
my recommendation and trudged along. I havn't time
to-day to tell you how I got along with the rest of the
editors, and a thousand other things that I met with
along by the way, and all the fine things in this great
city, and so on. But I shall write to you again soon.

Your loving neffu,

JACK DOWNING.

To Uncle Joshua Downing, Downingville, State of Maine.

LETTER XXVI.

*His visit to Major Noah, in New York, when he arriv-
ed there.*

Washington City, May 30, 1831.

To the Portland Courier, if it ever gets there, away down
   east in the State of Maine, to be sent to Uncle Joshua
   Downing, up in Downingville, with care and speed.

Dear Uncle Josh,—I've got here at last, to this
great city where they make offices, and I'm determined
not to leave it till I get one. It is n't sich a great city
after all as New York, though they do a great deal more
business here than they do at New York. I dont mean
vessel business and trade, for there's no end to that in
New York, but in making offices and sich like; and
they say its the most profitable business in the country.
If a man can get hold of a pretty good office, he can

get rich enough by it in three or four years, and not have to work very hard neither. I tell you what, uncle, if I make out to my mind here, I shall come back again one of these days in a rather guess way than what I come on. I dont have to foot it again I'll warrant you, and guess poor cousin Sally wont have to set up all night to mend my coat and darn my stockings. You'll see me coming dressed up like a lawyer, with a fine carriage and three or four hosses. And then them are chaps in Portland that used to laugh at me so about being Governor, may sneeze at me if they dare to, and if they dont keep out of my way I'll ride right over 'em. I had a pretty tuft time coming on here. Its a long tiresome road through the Jarseys. I had to stop twice to get my shoes tapt, and once to get an old lady to sow up a rip in my coat while I chopped wood for her at the door to pay for it. But I shant mind all the hard work I've had of it, if I can make out to come home rich.

I got a pretty good boost in Boston, as I writ you in my last, by the editors giving me recommendations.— But it was nothing at all hardly to what I got in New York, for they gave me a *public dinner* there. I cant think what's the matter that it hasn't been published yet. Major Noah promised me he'd have it all put into the New York Courier and Enquirer the very next day after I left New York, so that it should get to Washington as soon as I did; and now I've been here about a week and it hasn't come yet. If it does'nt come soon, I shall write an account of the dinner myself, and send it home and get it put in the Portland Courier. It was a most capital dinner, uncle; I dont know as I ever eat heartier in my life, for being pretty short of money I had pinched rather close a day or two, and to tell the truth I was as hungry as a bear. We had toasts and speeches and a great many good things. I dont mean sich toast as they put butter on to eat, but toast to drink. And they dont exactly drink 'em neither; but they drink the punch and speak the toasts.

I cant think Major Noah meant to deceive me about

publishing the proceedings of the dinner, for he appeared to be a very clever man, though he was the funniest chap that ever I see.   There was n't a man in New York that befriended me more than he did; and he talked to me very candidly, and advised me all about how to get an office. In the first place, says he, Mr. Downing, you cant get any kind of an office at Washington, unless you are a true blue ginuin democratic republican.   I told him I had recommendations coming to prove that I was all that. They are very strict, says he, in regard to that at Washington. If James Madison should apply for an office at Washington, says he, he could n't get it. What, says I, him that was President! for it kind of startled me a little if such an old republican as he was could n't get an office. It's true, says he, if James Madison should apply for an office he could n't get it.—Why not, says I? Because, says he, *he has turned federalist.* It's melancholy to think, says he, how many good old republicans at the south are turning federalists lately.   He said he was afraid there was n't more than one true ginuin old democratic republican left in Virginny, and that was old Mr. Ritchie of the Richmond Enquirer; and even he seemed to be a little wavering since Mr. Calhoun and some others had gone over.

Well there's Mr. Clay, says I, of Kentucky, I dont think he'll ever flinch from the republican cause. Henry Clay, says he, turning up his nose, why he's been a federalist this six years.   No, no, Mr. Downing, if you think of going that gate, you may as well turn about and go home again before you go any further.   What gate, says I ? Why to join the clay party, says he. I told him I never had sich a thought in my life ; I always belonged to the republican party, and always ment to. He looked rather good natured again when he heard that ; and says he, do you know what the true republican doctrine is ? I told him I had always had some kind of an idea of it, but I did n't know as I could explain it exactly. Well, says he, I'll tell you; it is to support General Jackson for re-election, through thick and thin. That is the only thing that will save the country from ruin. And if General Jackson should be unwell or any thing jest before election, so he could not be a candidate, the true republican doctrine is to support Mr. Van Buren. I told him, very well, he might depend upon my sticking to the republican party, all weathers. Upon that he set down and wrote me a recommendation to the President for an office, and it almost made me blush to see what a master substantial ginuin republican he made me. I had a number more capital recommendations at New York, but I hav n't time to tell you about them in this letter. Some were to Mr. Clay, and some to Mr. Van Buren, and some to Mr. Calhoun. I took 'em all, for I thought it was kind of uncertain whose hands I might fall into hereafter, and it might be well enough to have two or three strings to my bow.

I hav n't called on the President yet, though I've been here about a week. My clothes had got so shabby, I thought I better hire out a few days and get slicked up a little. Three of the offices that I come after are gone slick enough, and the other one's been given away to a Mr. White, but he would n't take it; so I 'm in hopes I shall be able to get it. And if I dont get that, there's some chance for me to get in to be Vice President, for they had a great Jackson meeting here 'tother day, and they kicked Mr. Calhoun right out doors, and said they would n't have him for Vice President no longer. Now some say they think I shall get it, and some think Mr. Van Buren 'll get it.

Howsomever, I feel pretty safe, for Maj. Noah told me if I could n't get any thing else, the President could easily make a foreign mission for me. I shall call on the good old Gineral in two or three days and find out what my luck is, and then I shall let you know. Give my love to ant and cousin Nabby, and all of 'em. It makes me feel kind of bad when I think how fur I've got from home.   Your loving neffu,
                    JACK DOWNING.

LETTER XXVII.

He arrives at Washington—strips up his sleeves—defends Mr. Ingham on the front steps of his door during the after-clap that followed the explosion of the Cabinet.

Washington City, June 21, 1831.

To the Portland Courier again away down there in the State of Maine, to be sent to Uncle Joshua Downing, up in Downingville, or close to Cousin Nabby, it is n't much matter which, being that some of it is about the ladies.

DEAR UNCLE JOSH.—It's pretty trying times here. They carry on so like the old smoker, I dont hardly know what to make of it. If I had n't said I would n't leave Washington till I got an office, I dont know but I should come back to Downingville and go to planting potatoes. Them are Huntonites and Jacksonites down there in Maine last winter were pretty clever sort of folks to what these chaps are here. Cause down there if they get ever so mad, they did n't do nothing but talk and jaw one another; but here if any body does n't do to suit 'm, fact they 'll up and shoot him in a minute. I did n't think getting an office was such dangerous kind of business, or I dont know as I should have tried it. Howsomever, it's neck or nothing with me now, and I must do something to try to get some money here, for I about as lieves die as to undertake to foot it away back again clear to the State of Maine. And as the folks have to go armed here, I want you to put my old fowling piece into the stage and send it on here as quick as possible. I hope you'll be as quick as you can about it. for if I get an office I shant dare to take it till I get my gun. They come pretty near having a shooting scrape here yesterday. The Telegraph paper said something about Mr. Eaton's wife. It was nothing that I should think they need to make such a fuss about; it only said that some of the ladies here refused to visit

her. But some how or other it made Mr. Eaton as mad
as a March hair. He declared he'd fight somebody, he
did n't care who.

The first man he happened to come at was Mr. Ingham. So he dared Mr. Ingham out to fight. Not to
box, as they do sometimes up in Downingville, but to
stand and shoot at each other. But Mr. Ingham
would n't touch to, and told him he was crazy. That
made Mr. Eaton ten times more mad than he was before; and he declared he'd flog him any how, whether
he was willing or not. So he got a gang of gentlemen
yesterday to go with him to the Treasury office where
Mr. Ingham does his writing, and waited there and in
a grog shop close by as much as two hours for a chance
to catch him and give it to him. Mr. Ingham was out
a visiting in the city, and when he got home his folks
told him what was going on, and begged him not to go
to the office for he would certainly be killed. Poh,
says he, do you think I'm afraid of them are blustering
chaps? There's more smoke than fire there, I can tell
ye; give me my pistols, it is time for me to go to the
office. Some of the ladies cried, and some almost
fainted away. But he pacified 'em as well as he could,
and then set out for the office, and three or four men
went with him, and I guess they carried something under their arms that would make daylight shine through
a feller pretty quick. And I guess the gang of gentlemen waiting for him begun to smell a rat, for they
cleared out pretty soon and never touched him. But
their courage came again in the evening, and this same
gang of gentlemen turned out to Mr. Ingham's house,
and threatened to burst the doors open and drag him
out by the hair of the head and skin him alive. I
thought this was carrying the joke rather too far, so I
tho't I'd put in my oar; for when I see any body run
too hard I cant help taking their part.

So I stepped on to Mr. Ingham's front door steps,
and threw my hat down, and rolled up my sleeves, and
spit on my hands; and by that time the chaps began to

stare at me a little. And now, says I, Major Eaton, this is quite too bad. A man's house is his castle. Here's Mr. Ingham in his house as peaceable as a lamb; he is n't a meddling with nobody, and you need n't think to drag him out here to-night, I can tell ye. If you really want to take a bit of a box, just throw away your powder and ball, and here's the boy for you. I'll take a fist or two with you and glad of the chance. You impudent scoundrel, says he, who are you? what business is it to you what I *done?* Clear out, or I'll send you where you ought to be long ago. Well, then, you'll send me into some good office, says I, for there's where I ought to have been more than two years ago. Well, says he, clear out, and up he come blustering along towards the steps. But I jest put my foot down, and doubled my fist, and now, says I, Major Eaton, it wont be healthy for you to come on to these steps to-night.

Says he, I'm going through that door whether or no. Says I, you dont go through this door to-night, without you pass over the dead body of *Jack Downing* of the State of Maine. My stars, when they heard that, they dropt their heads as quick as though they had been cut off, for they did n't know who I was before. Major Eaton and the whole gang of gentlemen with him turned right about and marched away as still a pack of whipped puppies. They were afraid I should have 'em all up before the President to-day, and have 'em turned out of office; for it's got whispered round the city that the President sets a great deal by me, and that I have a good deal of influence with him.

This morning Mr. Ingham started for Philadelphy. Before he left, he thanked me a thousand times for defending his house so well last night, and he wrote a letter to the President, telling him all about the scrape. I went a piece with him to see him safe out of the city on the great road towards Baltimore.

About my prospects for an office, I cant tell you yet how I shall come out. I've been in to see the President

a number of times, and he talks very favorable. I
have some chance to get in to be Secretary of War, if
old Judge White dont take it; and if I dont get that
the President says he 'll do the best he can for me.

I never had to be so strict a republican before in my
life as I've had to be since I've been here in order to
get the right side of the President. I'll tell you something about it in my next, and about my visits to the
President, and a good many other famous things here.

P. S.   Be sure and send the old gun as soon as possible.   Your loving neffu,
                        JACK DOWNING.

LETTER XXVIII.

*Mr. Downing made Captain in the United States army,
with orders to go to Madawaska, and protect the inhabitants.*

Washington City, the 20th day of Oct. 1831.

To the Portland Courier away down in the State of Maine, to
be sent to Uncle Joshua Downing up in Downingville, this
with care and speed, and dont let any body see it.

DEAR UNCLE JOSH,—I've got it at last as true as
you're alive, and now I dont keer a snap for the fattest
of 'em. I'll teach them are young chaps down to Portland that used to poke fun at me so because I did n't
get in to be Governor, that they must carry a better
tongue in their heads, or they 'll find out who they are
talking to. I guess they 'll find out by and by it wont
be healthy for 'em to poke fun at an officer of my rank.
And as for Jemime Parsons that married the school
master winter before last, when she had promised as
fair as could be that she would have me, she may go to
grass for what I keer; I would n't have her now no
more than I 'd have a Virginny nigger. And I guess

when she comes to see me with my regimentals on she
'll feel sorry enough and wish her cake was dough
again. Now she's tied down to that clodpole of a
school master, that was n't fit for a schoolmaster neither,
for he has had to go to hoeing potatoes for a living, and
much as ever he can get potatoes enough to keep 'em
from starving, when if she had only done as she had
promised, she might now be the wife of Captain Jack
Downing of the United States Army. But let her go;
as I said afore, I dont care a snap for her or all old
White's cattle. I'll tell you what 'tis uncle, I feel
about right now. It seems to me I could foot it home
in two days, for my feet never felt half so light before.
There's nothing like trying, in this world, uncle; any
body that tries can be something or other, if he dont get
discouraged too soon. When I came on here, you
know, I expected to get one of the great Secretaries'
offices ; but the good old President told me they had got
him into such a hobble about them are offices that he
could n't give me one of 'em if he was to die. But he
treated me like a gentleman, and I shall always vote for
him as long as I live, and I told him so. And when he
found out that I was a true ginuin republican, says he,
Mr. Downing, you must be patient, and I'll bear you in
mind, and do something for you the very first chance.
And you may depend upon it Mr. Downing, he added
with a good deal of earnestness, I never desert my
friends, let that lying Stephen Simpson of Philadelphy
say what he will about it, a good for nothing ungrateful
dog. And he fetched a stomp with his foot and his eyes
kind of flashed so fiery, that I cou'd n't help starting
back, for I did n't know but he was going to knock me
over. But he look'd pleasant again in a minute, and
took me my the hand, and now, says he, Mr. Downing,
I give you my honour that I'll do something for you as
soon as I possibly can. I told him I hoped he would be
as spry as he could about it, for I had but jest ninepence left, and I did n't know how I should get along
very well, in a strange place too. But he told me never

to mind that at all; I might come and eat my meals at his house whenever I'd a mind to, or he would be bondsman for my board where I put up. So I've worked along from that time to this, nearly for months, as well as I could, sometimes getting a little job of garden-work, and sometimes getting a little wood to saw, and so on, nearly enough to pay my expenses. I used to call and see the President once in a while, and he always told me I must be patient and keep up a good heart, the world was n't made in one day, and something would turn up for me by and by. But fact, after digging, and sawing, and waiting four months, my patience got most wore out, and I was jest upon the point of giving up the chase, and starting off for Downingville with the intention of retiring to private life; when last night, about seven o'clock, as I sot eating a bowl of bread and milk for my supper, a boy knocked at the door and wanted to see Mr. Downing. So they brought him into the room where I was, and says he, Mr. Downing, the President wants to see you for something very particular, right away this evening. My heart almost jump'd right up in my mouth. My spoon dropt out of my hand, and to eat another mouthful I could n't if I was to starve. I flew round, and washed my face and hands, and combed my head, and brushed up as well as I could, and should have looked tolerable spruce if it had n't been for an unlucky hole in the knee of my trowsers. What to do I did not know. It made me feel bad enough I can tell you. The woman where I boarded said she would mend them for me if I would take them off, but it would take her till about nine o'clock, and the President was waiting for me, and there 'twas. Such a hobble I never was in-before. But this woman is a kind good creature as ever was; she boards me for four and sixpence a week, considering that I split wood for her, and bring water, and do all sich kind of chores. And she always had some contrivance to get out of every difficulty; and so she handed me a neat little pocket handkerchief and told me to

tie that round my knee. Being thus rigged out at last,
I started off as fast as I could go for the President's.

When I went into his room, the old gentleman was
setting by a table with his spectacles on, and two great
lamps burning before him, and a bundle of letters and
papers in his hand. He started up and took me by the
hand, and says he, good evening Mr. Downing, I'm very
glad to see you; you are the very man I want now,
above all others in the world. But how is this, said he?
looking at my knee. Not lame, I hope? That would
be a most unfortunate thing in this critical moment. It
would knock my plan in the head at once. I felt kind
of blue, and I guess I blushed a little; but I turned it
off as well as I could; I told him I was n't lame at all,
it was nothing but a slight scratch, and by to-morrow
morning I should be as well as ever I was in my life.
Well then says he, Mr. Downing, set down here and see
what I've got to tell you. The old gentleman set himself back in his chair and pushed his spectacles up on
his forehead and held up the letter in his hand, and says
he, Mr. Downing, here is a letter from Governor Smith
of Maine, and now Sir, I've got something for you to
do. You see now that I was sincere when I told you
if you would be patient and stick to the republican text,
I would look out for you one of these days. I'm always true to my friends; that lying Stephen Simpson
might have had an office before now if he had behaved
himself.

Well, dear sir, said I, for I felt in such a pucker to
know what I was going to get that I could n't stand it
any longer, so says I, what sort of business is it you 've
got for me to do? Says he, Mr. Downing, I take it you
are a man of courage; I have always thought so ever
since you faced Mr. Eaton so boldly on Mr. Inghams'
door steps. Tho' I was sorry your courage was not dis-
played in a better cause, for that Ingham is a rascal after
all. I told him as for courage I believed I had some of
the stuff about me when there was any occasion for it,
and that I never would stand by and see any body

abused. Well, says he, we must come to the point, for the business requires haste.

Governor Smith writes me that there are four of your fellow citizens of Maine in a British jail at Fredericton, who have been taken from their farms by British constables and sheriffs and other officers and carried off by force to prison. By this time my very hair begun to curl, I felt so mad, and I could n't help jumping up and smiting my fists together, and saying pretty hard things about the British Well, says the President, I like your spunk Mr. Downing; you're jest the man I want in this business. I 'm going to give you a captain's commission in the United States' army, and you must go down there and set that business right at Madawaska.

You must go to Maine and raise a company of volunteers as quick as possible, tell 'em I 'll see 'em paid, and you must march down to Fredericton and demand the prisoners, and if they are not given up you must force the jail, and if the British make any resistance you must fire upon them and bring the prisoners off at some rate or other. Then write me and let me know how affairs stand, and I 'll give you further orders. At any rate you must see that the rights of Maine are well protected, for that state has come round so in my favor since last year I 'm determined to do every thing I can for them; I tell you Mr. Downing, I never desert my friends. So after he gave me the rest of my orders, and my commission, and a pocket full of money, and told me to be brave and if I wanted any thing to let him know, he bid me good night, and I went home. But I could n't sleep a wink all night. I was up before day light this morning, and I 've got two women to work for me to day fixing up my clothes, and I shall be ready to start to morrow morning. I want you to keep this matter pretty still till I get there, except that you may let cousin Ephraim know it and get him to volunteer some of the Downingville boys for my company. I want to get them pretty much all there if I can, for I know what

G

sort of stuff the Downingville boys are made of, and shall know what I 've got to depend upon.

In haste, your loving neffu,

CAPT. JACK DOWNING.

LETTER XXIX.

First military report of Capt. Downing to the president.

Downingville, Nov. 8, 1831.

To the Editor of the Portland Courier.

My dear old Friend, you.—I got home to Downingville last night after an absence of nearly two years. I meant to stop at Portland as I come on from Washington, but some how or other, I got into the wrong stage somewhere in New Hampshire, and come the upper road before I knew it. So the first thing I knew, when I thought I had got almost to Portland, I found myself plump in Downingville. But the dear folks were all so glad to see me, I didn't feel much sorry. Cousin Nabby hopped right up and down, like a mouse treed in a flour barrel; and Ephraim snapped his thumb and finger, and spit on his hands as though he had a cord of wood to chop; and poor ant Keziah set down and cried as much as two hours steady. Uncle Joshua catched down his pipe, and made the smoke roll out well; I never saw him smoke so fast before in my life; he finished two pipes full of tobacco in less than five minutes. I felt almost like a fool myself, and had to keep winking and swallowing, or I should have cried as hard as any of 'em. But you know it wouldn't do for a captain to cry, especially when he was going to enlisting soldiers.

Well, I must hurry along with my letter, for I have n't got much time to write to-day. I have been round

among the folks in Downingville this forenoon to see
how they felt about the Madawaska business, and whether any of 'em would go a sogering down there with
me. I find some of 'em are right up about it, and
ready to shoulder their guns and march to-morrow if I
say the word, and others are a little offish.

I guess I shall get about half enough for a company
here pretty easy, and if I find it hard dragging to pick
up the rest, I shall come right down to Portland to fill
up my company there. For uncle Joshua tells me he
has had some letters from Portland within a few days,
and he says there are a number of chaps down there as
warm as mustard about going to war down to Madawaska, and are only waiting for a good chance to list,
and some of 'em he thinks will make capital sargents
and corporals. I should be glad if you would send me
word whether you think I could pick up some good lusty
fellows there in case I should want 'em. I pay a month's
wages cash down. But there is one subject that I feel
rather uneasy about, and that is the greatest reason of
my writing you to-day, to see if you can tell me any
thing about it. Last night uncle Joshua and I sot up
talking politicks pretty late, after all the rest of the
folks had gone to bed. I told him all about one thing
or another at Washington, and then we talked about
the affairs of this State.

I found uncle Joshua did't stand jest where he used
to. You know once he was a little mite in favor of
Mr. Hunton ; and then, when I was up for Governor,
he was altogether in favour of me ; and then he was
pretty near equally balanced between Mr. Smith and
Mr. Goodenow ; but now, when I come to talk with
him, I found he was all plump over on the democratic
republican side. You know I've been leaning that way
tu, ever since I got in to be good friends long with President Jackson. So says I, Well, uncle, our party is
strong enough now to carry all afore 'em in this State.
I guess governor Smith will have more than three quarters of the votes next time. At which uncle turned

round towards me, and rolled up his great eyes over his spectacles, and took his pipe out of his mouth and put on a mighty knowing look, and says he, Jack, jest between you and me, *a much better man and a much greater republican than Gov. Smith, will be Governor of the State of Maine after another election.*

I was kind of struck with a dunderment. I sot and looked at him as much as two minutes, and he all the time looked as knowing as a fox. At last, says I, Uncle, what do you mean ? Did n't all the democratic republican papers in the State, when Gov. Smith was elected, say he was the very best republican there was in the State for Governor. Well, well, Jack, said he, mark my words, that 's all. But, said I, uncle, what makes you think so ? O, said he, I have read the Argus and the Bangor Republican, and I have had a letter from a man that knows all about it, and when the time comes you 'll see. And that was all I could get out of him. Now I wish you would let me know what this mystery means. And I remain your old friend,

CAPT. JACK DOWNING.

LETTER XXX.

The first military report of Capt. Downing to the President.

Madawaska, Nov. 15, 1831.

To his Excellency, Gineral Jackson, President of the United States, &c.

MY GOOD OLD SIR.—The prisoners are out and no blood spilt yet. I had prepared to give the British a most terrible battle, if they had n 't let ' em out. I guess I should made 'em think old Bonapart had got back among 'em again, for a keener set o fellows than my company is made up of never shouldered a musket or trod shoe-leather. I was pesky sorry they let 'em out quite as soon, for I really longed to have a brush with 'em ; and how they come to let 'em go I dont know, unless it was because they heard I was coming. And I expect that was the case, for the prisoners told me the British Misnister at Washington, sent on some kind of word to Governor Campbell, and I suppose he told him how I had got a commission, and was coming down upon New Brunswick like a hurrycane.

If I could only got down there a little sooner and fite sich a great battle as you did at New Orleans, my fortune would have been made for this world. I should have stood a good chance then to be President of the United States, one of these days. And that's as high as ever I should want to get. I got home to Downingville in little more than a week after I left you at Washington, for having a pretty good pocket full of money, and knowing that my business was very important, I rid in the stage most all the way. I spose I need n't stop to tell you how tickled all my folks were to see me. I did n't know for awhile but they'd eat me up. But I spose that's neither here nor there in making military reports, so I'll go on. I found no difficulty in getting volunteers. I believe I could have got nearly half the State of Maine to march if I had wanted 'em. But as I only had orders to list one good stout company, I took 'em all in Downingville, for I rather trust myself with one hundred ginuin Downingville boys, than five hundred of your common run. I took the supernumerary however, when I got to Bangor. The editor of the Bangor Republican was so zea ous to go, and said he'd fight so to the last drop of his blood, that I could n't help taking him, so I appointed him supernumerary corporal. Poor fellow, he was so disappointed when he found the prisoners were out that he fairly cried for vexation. He's for having me go right on now and give all New Brunswick a real thrashing.

But I know what belongs to gineralship better than

G 2

that; I have n't had my orders yet. Well, after we
left Bangor we had a dreadful rough and tumble sort of
a journey, over rocks and mountains and rivers and
swamps and bogs and meadows, and through long pieces
of woods that I didn't know as we should find the way
out. But we got through at last, and arrived here at
Madawaska day before yesterday. I thought I better
come this way and make a little stop at Madawaska to
see if the prisoners' wives and little ones were in want
of any thing and then go down to Fredericton and blow
the British ski high.

When our company first came out in sight in Madawaska, they thought it was the British coming to catch
some more of 'em; and such a scattering and scampering I guess you never see. The men flew into the
woods like a flock of sheep with forty dogs after 'em,
and the women catched their babies up in their arms
and run from one house to another screeching and
screaming enough to make the woods ring again. But
when they found out we were United States troops
come to help 'em, you never see any body so glad.—
They all cried for joy then. The women run into the
woods and called to their husbands to come back again,
for there was nobody there that would hurt them, and
back they came and treated us with the best they had in
their houses. And while we sot chatting, before the
women hardly got their tears wiped up, one of 'em
looked up towards the woods and screamed out *there
comes the prisoners.* Some turned pale a little, thinking it might be their ghost, but in a minute in they come,
as good flesh and blood as any of us, and then the women had another good crying spell.

I asked one of the prisoners how they got away, for
I thought you would want to know all about it; and says
he we come away on our legs. Did you break out of
jail, said I? I guess there was no need of that, said he,
for we want locked in half the time. Did you knock
down the guard, said I, and fight your way out?—
Humph! said he, I guess we might have hunted one

while before we could find a guard to knock down.
Nobody seemed to take any care of us, if we wanted a
drop of grog we had to go out and buy it ourselves.—
Well but, said I, if you were left in such a loose state
as that, why did you not run away before? Tut, said
he, shrugging up his shoulders, I guess we knew what
we were about; the longer we staid there the more land
the state of Maine would give us to pay us for being
put in jail, but when they turned us out of jail, and
would n't keep us any longer, we thought we might as
well come home.

And now, my good old sir, since matters are as they
are, I shall take up my head quarters here at Madawaska
for the present, and wait for further orders. I shall
take good care of the people here, and keep every thing
in good order, and not allow a single New Brunswicker
to come any where within gun-shot. As for that Lef-
tenant Governor, Mr. Archibald Campbell, he better
keep himself scarce ; if he shows his head here again,
I shall jest put him into a meal bag and send him to
Washington. I shall expect to hear from you soon, and
as I shall have to be here sometime, I dont know but you
had better send me on a little more money. My uniform got rather shattered coming through the woods,
and it will cost me something to get it fixt up again.

This from your old friend and humble servant,

CAPT. JACK DOWNING.

LETTER XXXI.

The Captain's second visit to the Maine Legislature.

Augusta, State of Maine, Jan. 4, 1832.

To the Editor of the Portland Courier.

MY DEAR OLD FRIEND,—Here I am right among the
Legislater folks, jest as I used to be down there to

Portland. I got here last night after a pretty hard journey from Madawaska, rather lame, and my feet and ears froze pretty bad. I hope I shant lose any of 'm, for if I should lose my feet I should n't stand much of a fag with the British down there to Fredericton in case we should have a brush with 'em. And all my hopes about ever being President of the United States depends on the woful whipping I'm going to give the British. And I'm afraid I should n't be much better off if I should lose my ears, for a President without ears would cut rather a sorry figure there to Washington. I sent on to the old President to see if he would let me have a furlough to come up to Augusta, while the Legislaters were here, for I thought I could n't stan it without being here to see how they get along. The President said he did n't think there would be any fighting down to Madawaska before the spring opens, so he did n't care if I went. I jest hobbled into the Legislater to-day to see 'em chuse officers; but I have n't any time to tell you what a great fine house they 've got into. I believe it 's vastly better than the one they had to Portland though. And I guess there 'll be no stopping the wheels of government this year, for I believe they have got the house fixed so as to carry the wheels by *steam*. They got the steam up before I went in, and it was so thick sometimes, that I should think the wheels might go like a buzz.

They told me there was a good many new members, and a good many more of 'em, than there was last year; so I did n't know as I should see hardly any body that I knew. But I never was more agreeably disappointed in my life than I was by the first voice I heard calling the members to order.

I knew it as quick as I could tell the fife and drum of my own company at Madawaska. And if I should hear the fife and drum this very minute it would n't give a pleasanter thrill to my feelings. I look'd round and sure enough there was the sandy honest look, and the large fleshy figure, of my old friend Mr. Knowlton

of Montville, holding a broad brimmed hat in his hand,
and calling upon the great jam of folks to come to order. I could n't hardly help crowding right in among
'em to shake hands with him, I was so glad to see him.
But as I was only a lobby member I tho't it would n't
do.

But I 'll tell you what 'it is, you may depend upon
the business going off glibb here this winter; for having a building go by steam and Mr. Knowlton here to
drive it, it aint all the Jacksonites and Huntonites in
the state that can stop it.   And besides I cant find out
as yet that there is any more than one party here; if
there should be hereafter, I 'll let you know. I was
glad they chose Mr. White to be speaker, for he's always so good natured and uses every body so well, I
cant help liking him.   I have n't been in the Sinnet
yet, but they say Mr. Dunlap is President. I was in
hopes to see Elder Hall here this winter, but I believe
he has n't come.

Your old Friend,
CAPT. JACK DOWNING.

LETTER XXXII.

The Legislative proceedings described.

Augusta, State of Maine, Jan. 19, 1832.

To the Editor of the Portland Courier.

MY DEAR OLD FRIEND,—If I could n't write to you
once in a while, I don't know but I should die. When
any thing has kept me from writing two or three weeks,
I get in such a taking it seems as though I should split,
and the only way I can get relief is to take my pen and
go at it.   The reason why you have n't heard from me
this fortnight past, is this dreadful furenza.   We've all

got it here, and it's nothing but cough, cough, the whole
time.   If a member gets up to speak, they all cough at
him.   If he says any thing that they like, they cough
at it; and if he says any thing that they dont like, they
cough at it   So let him say what he will they keep a
steady stream of coughing.   I've been amost sick for a
week.   Some days I want hardly able to set up.   But
I'm getting cleverly now, and I hope I shall be able to
let you hear from me once or twice a week during the
session.

The wheels of government go pretty well this winter.
Some say that some folks have tried to trig 'em two or
three times, but I dont hardly think that is the case, for
they havn't been stopt once.   And, as I said in my last
letter, if my friend Mr. Knowlton stands as foreman,
and keeps his broad shoulders to the wheels, I dont believe they will stop this winter.   By the way, I made
a little small mistake about Mr. Knowlton's hat.   I
should n't have thought it worth while to mention it
again, if the Augusta Courier of this morning had n't
spoke of it as though I did n't mean to tell the truth.
Now you know Mr. Editor, I would n't be guilty of
telling a falsehood for my right hand.   When Mr.
Knowlton called the members to order the first day of
the session, I certainly thought I saw him holding in
his hand a broad brimmed white hat.   It might be my
imagination, remembering how he used to look, or it
might possibly be the hat of the member standing by
the side of him, for I was a good ways off.

I'm pesky fraid the general government may settle
that hash down there to Madawaska as Mr. Netherlands that they left out to, recommended.   If they
should I'm afraid my jig would be up about fighting a
battle very soon, or getting in to be President.

Our party's got into a dreadful kind of a stew here
about who shall be next Senator to Congress and one
thing or another.   We've got into such a snarl about it,
I'm afraid we never shall get unravelled again without
cutting off the tangles, and that would divide us so we

never could hold together in the world. I wrote to the Argus yesterday, to be sure not to reply to the Age for its ungentlemanly remarks about Judge Preble, and hope it will be prudent enough to follow my recommendation. We must try to hush these matters up, or it 'll be the death of the party. I've had a serious talk with friend Ruggles, and am in hopes he'll put his hand over the Thomaston paper and not let it belch out any thing that our enemies can make a handle of. And I guess we shall have a caucus and try to put a cooler on the Bangor Republican and the Age.

The Legislaters like Augusta considerable well, if it did n't cost 'em so much more than it did in Portland for a living. Such as had to pay two dollars and a half in Portland for board have to pay three and four dollars here. When I was in Portland, I used to get boarded for seven and sixpence a week, and here the cheapest I could get boarded any where, was ten and sixpence. The Augusta Courier last week said something about the folks here giving me a public dinner. I should like it pretty well, for I have rather slim dinners where I board.

If you see cousin Sally, I wish you'd jest ask her if she has time before and after school, if she'll knit me a pair of footings and send 'em up by the stage-driver, for mine have got pretty full of holes, and I have n't any body here to mend 'em.

Your old friend,
CAPT. JACK DOWNING.

LETTER XXXIII.

The captain suddenly called to his post at Madawaska.

Augusta, State of Maine, Jan. 23, 1832.

To the Editor of the Portland Courier, again.

DEAR FRIEND,—The more I write to you, it seems to me the better I like you. I believe there is n't but one person that I set so much by, and that is Gineral Jackson, who was so kind as to give me a commission, and let me have spending money besides. I 'm pretty much out of money now, and the man that I board with keeps dunning me for pay ; so I wish you would be so kind as t᷎ send me four or five dollars till I get some more from the President. I writ for it last week, and I think I shall get it in a few days. I told you in my last letter, if I got over the furenza, you should hear from me pretty often. I 'm getting nicely again now. I dont cough more than once in five minutes or so, and my toes and ears that were froze so bad coming up from Madawaska are nearly healed over. All I have to do to 'em now is jest to grease 'em a little when I go to bed at night and in the morning when I get up. I have to keep a handkerchief over my ears yet when I go out, but my toes are so well I dont limp hardly a mite. As to our legislater business we get along middling well, but not quite so fast as I thought we should considerin it goes by steam. One reason I suppose is because Mr. Knowlton has been a good deal unwell and could n't take hold and drive it right in end as he used to. But he 's got better now, so I hope the wheels will begin to buzz again.

About the quarrel that our party's got into, I 'm pesky fraid it 'll blow us up yet ; and I don't know what we shall do to stop it. We 've had a caucus as I told you we should in my last letter, and tried to hush matters up as well as we could. But some of 'em are so grouty, I expect nothing but what they 'll belch out again.

I was glad the Argus took my advice and kept back the reply to the Age.

We had a little bit of a tussle here to see who should be appointed agent to go to Washington to tell the president to hold on to the territory down to Madawaska. Mr. Preble and Mr. Deane and I were the three principal candidates. Some thought Mr. Preble ought to go because it would be for the interest of the republican party ; and some thought Mr. Deane ought to go because he had been down there a good deal and knew all about the Madawaska country ; and some thought I ought to go because I had been down there the last of any body, and because I was such good friends with the President I should be likely to do better than any body else could. I thought my claims were the strongest, and the Governor said he thought so too. But he said as affairs now stood it would n't do to appoint any body but Mr. Preble.

And besides I dont know as I ought to go off jest now, for I had a letter yesterday from one of my subalterns down to Madawaska, that there 's some trouble with my company there : some of the Sarjeants been breaking orders, &c., and I dont know but I shall have to go down and Court Martial 'em.

Your friend,
CAPT. JACK DOWNING

LETTER XXXIV.

*His return o Augusta—is saved from being frozen to
death by a bear's skin.*

Augusta, State of Maine, Feb. 8, 1832.

To the Editor of the Portland Courier.

HERE I be again, my dear friend, right back on
the old spot, poking about the Legislater to see what's
going on, and to help take care the interests of our
party. I got down there to Madawaska jest in the
nick of time ; for I got a hoss and rid day and night ;
and it was well I did, for Sargant Joel had got so outrageous mad, I raly believe if I had n't got there the
day I did, he would have strung one or two of 'em
right up by the neck. But I quashed matters at once
and sot 'em to studyin that are little court martial book,
and told 'em when they had any more fuss, they must
try all their cases by that, and they would n't find any
law for hanging in it.

It 's dreadful cold down there to Madawaska, I froze
my toes and ears agin, a little, but not so bad as I did
afore, for I took care to rop up in a great bear skin. I
see the Legislater's been disputing about passing a
law to kill off all the bears and wolves and sich kind
of critters.

I dont know whether that's a good plan or not.—
There's a good deal might be said on both sides.—
Them are bears are pesky mischievous. I heard a
story while I was gone, but I dont know how true it is,
how a great bear chased the Councillor that the Governor sent down to Frederickton, to carry provisions to
our prisoners in jail there. Some reckoned the bear
smelt the bread and cheese that he had in his saddle
bags, and so took after him to get some of it. However, the Councillor got back safe. But I think this is

a great argument in favour of killing off all the bears. And on the other hand, I believe the bear skin was all that kept me from freezing to death going to Madawaska t'other day. So it seems we ought not to kill 'em quite all off, but raise enough to keep us in bear skins; for I suppose my life would be worth as much to the State as the Councillor's.

I feel a little put out with Dr. Burnham for an unhandsome running he gave me t'other day in the Senate. He called me an 'old rogue.' I cant swallow that very well ; for that's a character I never bore in Downingville, nor Washington nor any where else. He was disputing about paying Mr. Deane and Mr. Cawano for going to Madawaska. He said they had n't ought to pay so much, for if they went on at this rate, next thing that old rogue, Capt. Jack Downing, would be sending in his bill.

But he need n't trouble himself about that, for as long as I have President Jackson to look to for paymaster, I dont care a snap about sending in my bills to to Legislater. But as for being called an old rogue, I wont: I dont mean to make a great fuss about it in the papers, as the Argus, and the Age did, so as to break up the harmony of the republican party. But if Dr. Burnham dont give me satisfaction, I'll call a caucus of the party and have him over the coals and du him over.

Your loving friend,
CAPT. JACK DOWNING.

LETTER XXXV.

*The Captain describes the manner in which the Legis-
lature makes Lawyers.*

Augusta, State of Maine, March 1st, 1832.

To the Editor of the Portland Courier.

MY DEAR OLD FRIEND,—I begin to feel as uneasy
as a fish out of water, because I havn't writ to you for
most two weeks. Now, old March has come, and
found us digging here yet; and sometimes I'm most
afraid we shall be found digging here, when we ought
to be at home digging potatoes, or planting of 'em at
least. I've been waiting now above a week for the
Legislater to do something, that I could write to you
about; but they dont seem to get along very smart lately. Sometimes the wheels almost stop; and then they
start and rumble along a little ways. and then drag
again. I dont think we shall get through before sometime next week, if we do before week arter. These
secret sessions take up a good deal of time. I dont see
what in natur they have so many of 'em for. I tried to
get into some of 'em, but they wouldn't let me; they
said lobby members had no business there, and shut
the door right in my face. There's one kind of business though that they carry on here pretty brisk lately,
and that is *making lawyers.* Some days they make
'em almost as fast as uncle Ephraim used to make sap-
troughs; and I've known him to chop off and hew out
two in fifteen minutes.

But for all the Legislater can make 'em so fast, it is
as much as ever they can get along with all that come
and want to be made over into lawyers. And 'tother
day, when the law committee got pretty well stuck,
having so many of 'em on hand, a new batch come up,
and Mr. Hall of your town moved to refer them to the
committee on *manufactures.* This is a capital committee to make things, and I havn't heard any com-

plaint since, but what they can turn 'em out as fast as they come. It rather puzzled me at first to know what made every body want to be worked over into lawyers; so I asked one of 'em that stood waiting round here a day or two, to be put into the hopper and ground over, what he wanted to be made into a lawyer for? And he kind of looked up one side at me, and give me a knowing wink, and says he, don't you know that the law yers get all the fat things of the land, and eat out the insides of the oisters, and give the shels to other folks? And if a man wants to have any kind of an office, he can't get it unless he's a lawyer; if he wants to go to the Legislater, he can't be elected without he's a lawyer: and if he wants to get to Congress, he cant go without he's a lawyer; and any man that don't get made into a lawyer as fast as possible, I say, is a fool. The whole truth come across my mind then, as quick as a look, why it was that I spent two or three years trying to get an office, and couldn't get one. It was because I wasn't a lawyer. And dont believe I should have got an office to this day, if my good friend President Jackson hadn't found out I was a brave two fisted chap, and just the boy to go down to Madawaska and flog the British.

We've agreed *unanimously* to support Governor Smith for re-election; and he'll come in all hollow, let the Jacksonites and Huntonites say what they will about it. Our party know too well which side their bread is buttered, to think of being split up this heat. I should write you more to day, but I feel so kind of agitated about these secret sessions, that I cant hardly hold my pen still. I'm a little afraid they are intriguing to send on to the President to take my commission away from me. It has been thrown out to me that I ought to be down to Madawaska, instead of being here all winter. Some have hinted to me that Mr. Clifford has taken a miff against me, because the other day when he was chosen Speaker pro. tem. one of my friends voted for me ; and he thinks I was a rival can-

H 2

didate, and means to have me turned out of office if he
can.   I am your loving friend,

CAPT. JACK DOWNING.

LETTER XXXVI.

*The Major's troubles on learning that the Legisla-
tures' resolution to sell Madawaska to the general government, to be bargained to the British, calculates
by figures its price—the rage of his men on learning
that they would have no fighting before parting with
it.*

Madawaska, State of Maine, or else Great Britain, I
dont know which, March 12, 1832.

*To the Editor of the Portland Courier—this with care
and speed.*

MY DEAR OLD FRIEND,—I cleared out from Augusta
in such a kind of a whirlwind, that I had n't time to
write you a single word before I left.   And I feel so
kind of crazy now, I dont know hardly which end I
stand upon.   I've had a good many head-flaws and
worriments in my life time, and been in a great many
hobbles, but I never, in all my born days,met with any
thing that puzzled me quite so bad as this ere *selling
out* down here.   I fite in the I egislater as long as fighting would do any good, that is, I mean in the caucus,
for they would n't let me go right into the Legislater in
the day time and talk to 'em there, because I was only
a lobby member.   But jest let them know it, lobby
members can do as much as any on 'em on sich business as this.   I laid it down to 'em in the caucus as
well as I could.   I asked 'em if they did n't think I
should look like a pretty fool, after marching my compa-

ny down there, and standing ready all winter to flog the whole British nation the moment any on 'em set a foot on to our land, if I should now have to march back again and give up the land, and all, without flogging a single son-of-a-gun of 'em. But they said it was no use, it could n't be helped, Mr. Netherlands had given away the land to the British, and the President had agreed to do jest as Mr. Netherlands said about it, and all we could do now was to get as much pay for it as we could.

So I set down and figured it up a little to see how much it would come to, for I used to cypher to the rule of three when I went to school, and I found it would come to a pretty round sum. There was, in the first place, about two millions of acres of land. This, considerin the timber there was on it, would certainly be worth a dollar an acre, and that would be two millions of dollars. Then there was two or three thousand inhabitants, say twenty-five hundred; we must be paid for them too, and how much are they worth ? I've read in the newspapers that black slaves at the south, sell for three or four hundred dollars apiece. I should think, then, that white ones, ought to fetch eight hundred. This, according to the rule of three, would be two hundred thousand dollars. Then, there's the pretty little town of Madawaska that our Legislater made last winter, already cut and dried with town officers all chosen, and every thing ready for the British to use without any more trouble. We ought to have pay for this too, and I should think it was worth ten thousand dollars.

And then the town of Madawaska has chosen Mr. Lizote to be a representative in the Legislater, and as the British can take him right into the Parliament without choosing him over again, they ought to pay us for that too. Now I have read in the newspapers that it sometimes costs, in England, two hundred thousand dollars to choose a representative to Parliament, reckoning all the grog they drink and all the money they

pay for votes.   But I wouldn't be screwing about it, so
I put Mr. Lizote down at one hundred thousand dollars.   And then I footed up, and found it to be,—

For land, including timber, two millions of
    dollars, $2,000,000
For inhabitants, including women and chil-
    dren, two hundred thousand dollars,   200,000
For town of Madawaska, officers and all,
    ten thousand dollars,   10,000
For Mr. Lizote, all ready to go to Parlia-
    ment, one hundred thousand dollars,   100,000
                                              —————

          Total, $2,310,000

This was a pretty round sum, and I begun to think,
come to divide it out, it would be a slice a-piece worth
having; especially if we did't give the Feds any of it,
and I supposed we shouldn't as there wasn't any of 'em
there in the caucus to help to see about it.

'In this view of the subject,' I almost made up my
mind that we ought to be patriotic enough to give it
up, and help the general government out of the hobble
they had got into.   And I was jest a-going to get up
and make a speech and tell 'em so, when Mr. McCrate
of Nobleborough, and Capt. Smith of Westbrook, two
of the best fellers in our party, came along and see what
I was figuring about, and, says they, Capt. Downing.
are you going to sell your country?   In a minute I
felt something rise up in my throat, that felt as big as
an ox-yoke.   As soon as I got so I could speak, says
I, No, *never,* while my name is Jack Downing, or my
old rifle can carry a bullet.   They declared too, that
they wouldn't s*ell out* to the general government, nor
the British, nor nobody else.   And we stuck it out
most of the evening, till we found out how it was going,
and then we cleared out, and as soon as the matter was
fairly settled, I started off for Madawaska; for I was
afraid if my company should hear of it before I got
there, it would make a blow up among 'em, and I should
have to court-martial 'em.

When I first told 'em how the jig was up with us, that the British were going to have the land, without any fighting about it, I never see fellows so mad before in my life, unless it was Major Eaton at Washington when he sot out to flog Mr. Ingham. They said if they could only have had one good battle, they wouldn't care a snap about it, but to be played tom-fool with in this way they wouldn't bear it. They were so mad, they hopped right up and down, and declared they never would go back till they had been over to Fredericton and pulled the jail down, or thrashed some of the New Brunswick boys. But, after a while, I pacified 'em by telling 'em if we didn't get a chance to fight here, I rather thought we might away off to Georgia, for there was something of a bobbery kicking up, and if the President should want troops to go on there, I was very sure my company would be one of the first he would send for.

So here we are, lying upon our arms, not knowing what to do. I have written to the President, and hope to hear from him soon. If the land is to go, I want to know it in season to get off before it's all over ; for I'll be hanged if ever I'll belong to the British.

Your distrest friend,
CAPT. JACK DOWNING.

LETTER XXXVII.

The office of Mayor of Portland offered to Capt. Downing and declined.

Portland, State of Maine, April 10, 1832.

To the citizens of Portland.

WHEN I arrived in this city, last night, from Madawaska, jest after the hubbub was over about the election,

I was informed some of my friends in Ward No. 7, had voted for me for Mayor. I believe the votes are put in the papers long with the scattering votes, as I see they dont publish my name.

Now the upshot ont is, I cant take that are office, I've got so much other business to attend to. And so I take this opportunity to declare that *I absolutely decline being a candidate.* I have a great regard for the citizens of Portland, for it was they that first gave me a boost up towards an office, and I should be very glad to do any thing for 'em that I could; but I must beg to be excused from being Mayor this year.

I am with respect,

CAPT. JACK DOWNING.

LETTER XXXVIII.

The Captain's account of a confidential conversation with President Jackson, while travelling to Tennessee.

Washington City, October 20, 1832.

To the Editor of the Portland Courier, away down east in the State of Maine: [*O dear, seems to me I never shall get there again.*]

MY DEAR OLD FRIEND,—I have n't done any thing this three months that seemed so natural as to set down and write to you. To write the name of the *Portland Courier* raises my sperits right up. I makes me feel as if I was again talking with you, and uncle Joshua, and cousin Ephraim, and cousin Nabby, and ant Sally, and all of 'em. I and President Jackson got back here yesterday from Tennessee, where we've been gone most all summer. And a long journey we've had of it too. I thought that from here to Portland was a dreadful ways, but it's a great deal further to Tennessee. I did n't think before that our country was half so large as I find it is. It seems as if there was no end to it; for when we got clear to Tennessee the President said we want half way acrost it. I could n't hardly believe him, but he stood tu it we want. Why, says he, Jack, I've got the largest country in the world, and the hardest to govern tu. Say what you will of free governments, where folks will act pretty much as they are a mind to, it's the hardest work to administer it that ever I did. I had rather fight forty New Orleans battles than to govern this everlasting great country one year. There are so many, you see, want to have a finger in the pye, it's the most difficult business you can imagine. You thought you had a tough time of it, Jack, to take care of them are small matters down to Madawaska last winter, with your brave company of Downingville boys. But that's no more than a drop in the bucket to being President one month. I tell you, Jack, there is n't a monarch in Europe who has so hard a time of it as I have. There are so many cooks, the broth most always comes out rather bad. If I have to write a message, one must put in a sentence, and another a sentence, and another, till it gets so at last I can't hardly tell whether I've written any of it myself or not. And sometimes I have a good mind to throw it all in the fire and say nothing at all. But then again that wont do, for since I 've undertaken to be President, I must go through with it. And then there was such a pulling and hauling for offices along in the outset, it seemed as though they would pull me to pieces. If I gave an office to one, Mr. Ingham or Mr. Branch would be mad, and if I gave it to another Mr. Van Buren would n't like it, and if I gave it to another, perhaps Mrs. Eaton would make a plaguy fuss about it. One wanted me to do this thing and another wanted me to do that: and it was nothing but quarrel the whole time. At last Mr. Van Buren said he 'd resign, if I would turn the rest out. So I made a scattering

among 'em and turned 'em all out in a heap. All but
Mr. Lewis and Mr. Kendall who staid to give me
their friendly advice and help me through my trying
difficulties.

And then again to be so slandered as I have been in
the papers, it is enough to wear the patience of Job out.
And if I got a little angry at the contrariness of the
Senate, they must needs call me a 'roaring lion,' the
rascals. But that Senate did use me shamefully. The
very best nominations I made, they always rejected. To
think the stupid heads should reject Mr. Van Buren, decidedly the greatest man in the country, it was too provoking. Yes, Mr. Van Buren is the first man in this
country, and jest betw en you and me, Jack, he's the
only man in it that is well qualified to succeed me in the
government of this great nation of twenty-four republics.
And he must come in too, or the country wont be worth
a stiver, much longer. There's Clay, he would make
pretty work of it, if he should come in. Why, Jack,
he would gamble one half of the country away in two
years, and spend the other half in digging Canals and
building rail-roads; and when the funds in the Treasury failed he would go to the United States Bank and
get more.

Calhoun would break the Union to pieces in three
months if he was President. He's trying all he can
now to tear off something of a slice from it at the south.
And as for Wirt, he's a fiddling away with the Anti-
masons. Letting Anti-masonry alone, he's a pretty good
sort of a man; but he has n't energy enough to steer our
crazy ship of state in these stormy times. I would sooner
trust it in the hands of Mrs. Eaton than him. There's
no one fit for it but Mr. Van Buren; and if it was not
for getting him in I would n't have consented to stand
for another term.

But, my dear friend, by stopping to tell you some of
the conversation I and the President had along the road,
I have almost forgot to tell you any thing about myself
and the thousand things I met with on my journey. But

I can't write any more to-day. I expect to start from here on Monday on my way to Portland. You may hear from me a few times before I get there, as I shall stop along by the way some to see how matters go in Pennsylvany and New York.

If you have a chance, send my love to all my folks up at Downingville, and tell 'em old Jack is alive and hearty.

I remain your loving friend,

CAPT. JACK DOWNING.

LETTER XXXIX.

The Captain's account of his having run express from Baltimore to Washington, with news from Pennsylvania, His interruptions by Gales and Duff Green, and his reception of and protection by the President.

Washington City, Nov. 5, 1832.

To the editor of the Portland Courier, in the Mariners' Church building, 2d story, eastern side, Fore Street, Portland, away down east, in the State of Maine.

MY DEAR OLD FRIEND.—Here I am back again to Washington, though I've been as far as Baltimore on my way down east to see you and the rest of my uncles and aunts and couzins. And what do you think I posted back to Washington for? I can tell you. When I got to Baltimore I met an *express* coming on full chisel from Philadelphy, to carry the news to Washington that Pennsylvania had gone all hollow for old Hickory's second election. The poor fellow that was carrying it had got out of breath, that he declared he couldn't go no further if the President never heard of it.

I

Well, thinks I, it will be worth a journey back to Washington, jest to see the old gineral's eyes strike fire when he hears of it. So says I, I'll take it and carry it on for you if you are a mind to. He kind of hesitated at first, and was afraid I might play a trick upon him; but when he found out my name was Jack Downing, he jumped off his horse quick enough; I'll trust it with you, says he, as quick as I would with the President himself. So I jumped on and whipped up. And sure enough, as true as you are alive, I did get to Washington before dark, though I had but three hours to go it in, and its nearly forty miles. It was the smartest horse that ever I backed, except one that belongs to the President. But, poor fellow, he's so done tu I guess he'll never run another express. Jest before I got to Washington, say about two miles from the city, the poor fellow keeled up and could n't go another step. I had lost my hat on the way and was too much in a hurry to pick it up, and he had thrown me off twice and torn my coat pretty bad, so that I did n't look very trig to go through the city or to the President's house. But notwithstanding, I knew the President would overlook it, considerin the business I was coming upon, so I catched the express and pulled foot, right through Pennsylvania Avenue, without any hat, and torn coat sleeves and coat tail flying. The stage offered to carry me, but I thought I wouldn't stop for it.

Almost the first person I met was Mr. Duff Green. Says he, Capt. Downing, what's the matter? I held up the express and shook it at him, but never answered him a word, and pulled on. He turned and walked as fast as he could without running, and followed me. Pretty soon I met Mr. Gales of the Intelligence., and says he, for mercy sake, Captain Downing, what's the matter? Have you been chased by a wolf, or Governor Houston, or have you got news from Pennsylvania?— I did n't turn to the right nor left, but shook the express at him and run like wild-fire.

When I came up to the President's house, the old gentleman was standing in the door. He stepped quicker than I ever see him before, and met me at the gate. Says he, my dear friend Downing, what's the matter? Has the United States Bank been trying to bribe you, and you are trying to run away from 'em? They may buy over Webster and Clay and such trash, but I knew if they touched you they would get the wrong pig by the ear. As he said this, Duff Green hove in sight, puffing and blowing, full speed.

Oh, said the President, Duff Green wants to have a lick at you, does he? Well dont retreat another step, Mr. Downing, I'll stand between you and harm. Upon that he called his boy and told him to bring his pistols in a moment. By this time I made out to get breath enough jest to say Pennsylvany, and to shake the express at him. The old man's colour changed in a minute. Says he, come in, Mr. Downing, come in, set down, dont say a word to Duff. So in we went, and shut the door. Now, says the President, looking as though he would rout a regiment in five minutes, now speak and let me know whether I am a dead man or alive.

Gineral, says I, its all over with —— I wont hear a word of it, says he, stomping his foot. His eyes flashed fire, so that I trembled and almost fell backwards. But I see he did n't understand me. Dear gineral, says I, its all over with Clay and the Bank—at that he clapt his hands and jumped up like a boy. I never see the President jump before, as much as I've been acquainted with him. In less than a minute he looked entirely like another man. His eyes were as calm and as bright as the moon jest coming out from behind a black thunder cloud.

He clenched my hand and gave it such a shake, I did n't know but he would pull it off. Says he, Jack, I knew Pennsylvany never would desert me, and if she has gone for me I'm safe. And now if I dont make them are Bank chaps hug it, my name is n't Andrew

Jackson. And after all, Jack, I aint so glad on my
own account, that I'm re-elected, as I am for the country and Mr. Van Buren's account; and we shall get
him in now to be President after me. And you know,
Jack, that he's the only man after me, that's fit to govern this country.

The President has made me promise to stop and
spend the night with him, and help him rejoice over the
victory. But I have n't time to write any more before
the mail goes.

Your loving friend,
CAPT. JACK DOWING.

LETTER XL.

*The captain commissioned as Major, and appointed to
march against the nullifiers.*

Washington City, Dec. 8, 1832.
To the Editor of the Portland Courier, in the Mariners' Church
building, second story, eastern end, Fore Street, Portland,
away down east, in the State of Maine.

MY DEAR OLD FRIEND.—I believe the last time I
wrote to you, was when I come back with the express
from Baltimore, and Duff Green chased me so through
the street to find out what I was bringing, and the President thought he was running to get a lick at me, and
called for his pistols to stand between me and harm,
you know. Well, I intended to turn right about again
after I had made the old gentleman's heart jump up by
telling him that he had got Pennsylvany and would be
elected as sure as eggs was bacon. and make the best of
my way towards Portland. For you cant think how I
long to see you and uncle Joshua and ant Kesiah and
cousin Ephraim and cousin Nabby and all the rest of

the dear souls up in Downingville. It seems as though it was six years instead of six months since I left that part of the country, and when I shall be able to get back again is more than I can tell now ; for I find when a man once gets into public life he never can say his time is his own ; he must always stand ready to go where his country calls. The long and the short of it is, the President has got so many other fish for me to fry, it's no use for me to think of going home yet. That evening after I got back with the express, the president said we must honor this victory in Pennsylvany with a glass of wine. I am sure, said he, Capt. Downing, you will have no objection to take a glass with me on this joyful occasion. I told him, as for that matter, I supposed I could take a glass of wine upon a pinch, even if the occasion was not half so joyful. So he had two or three bottles full brought in, and filled up the glasses. And now, says the president, I will give you a toast. The state of Pennsylvania, the most patriotic state in the Union ; for though I go against all her great public interests, still she votes for me by an over-whelming majority.

He then called for my toast. And what could I give but my near native Downingville ; the most gi-nuin unwavering democratic republican town in New England.

Good, said the president ; and that Downingville has never been rewarded yet. You shall have a post office established there, and name to me which of your friends you would like should be post-master, and he shall be appointed.

The president then gave his second toast ; Martin Van Buren, the next president of the United States, and the only man in the country that is fit for it. Capt. Downing, your toast if you please. So I gave Uncle Joshua Downing, the most thorough going republican in Downingville.

Good, said the president, I understand you, Captain Downing ; your uncle Joshua shall have the post office.

2 I

His third toast was the editor of the Washington Globe ; and mine was the editor of the Portland Courier. But I told him he mustn't ask me for any more toasts, for that was as fur as I could go.

The president toasted several more of his friends, sich as Major Eaton, and Mr. Kendall, and Mr. Lewis, and the Hon. Isaac Hill, and so on, till it got to be pretty late in the evening, and I told the president I would be glad if he would excuse me, for I wanted to start early in the morning on my way down East, and I thought I should feel better if I could get a little nap first. And besides I had got to go and get the old lady that used to do my washing and mending, to patch up my coat that got such a terrible shipwreck by being thrown off the horse with the express.

Start down East to-morrow morning, Capt. Downing, said he, you must not think of it. I have an important and delicate job on hand which I cant get along with very well without your assistance. There's that miserable ambitious Calhoun has been trying this dozen years to be president of the United States ; but he can't make out, so now he is determined to lop off a few of the southern states and make himself president of them. But if he don't find himself mistaken my name is n't Andrew Jackson. As he said this he started up on his feet, and begun to march across the floor with a very soldier-like step, and his eyes fairly flashed fire. No, said he, Capt. Downing, he must wait till somebody else is president besides me before he can do that. Let him move an inch by force in this business, if he dares. I 'll chase him as far as beyond Tennessee as it is from here there, but what I'll catch him and string him up by the neck to the first tree I can find.

I must send some troops out there to South Carolina to reconnoitre and keep matters strait, and your gallant defence of Madawaska last winter points you out as the most suitable man to take the command. I shall give you a major's commission to-morrow, and wish you to enlist two or three companies of brave volunteers and hold yourself in readiness to obey orders. In case we should have to come to a real brush, said the president, shall take command myself, and make you lieutenant-general. But I wish you to bear in mind, let what will come, never to shoot that Calhoun. Shooting is too good for him. He must dance upon nothing, with a rope round his neck.

As for your coat, Capt. Downing, dont trouble the old lady with it. It looks as though it had seen service enough already. I'll give you one of mine to wear till you have time to get a suit of regimentals made. I told him I felt a little uneasy about taking the command among strangers, unless I could have my Downingville company with me. Send for them, said the president, by all means, send for them. There are no troops equal to them except it is some of the boys from Tennessee. So I shall forthwith send orders to Sargeant Joel to march 'em on here. As I am to have my commission to-morrow, I shall venture to subscribe myself your friend,

MAJOR JACK DOWNING.

LETTER XLI.

Uncle Joshua's account of the tussle at Downingville in endeavouring to keep the Federalists from praising the president's anti-nullifying Proclamation.

Downingville, State of Maine, Dec. 27, 1832.

To Major Jack Downing, at Washington City, or if he is gone to South Carolina I want President Jackson to send this along tu him.

MY DEAR NEFFU,—We had almost gin you up for dead, you had been gone so long, before we got your letter in the Portland Courier telling how you had been away to Tennessee along with President Jackson.

Your poor mother had pined away so that she had
nothing left, seemingly, but skin and bones, and your
cousin Nabby had cried her eyes half out of her head,
poor girl. But when the Portland Courier came bringing that are letter of yourn, Downingville was in a
complete uproar all day. Sargent Joel had come home
from Madawaska and dismissed your company, and gone
to work in the woods chopping wood. But as soon as
he heard your letter had come, he dropped his ax, and I
dont think he's touched it since ; and he put on his
regimentals and scoured up the old piece of a scythe
that he used to have for a sword, and stuck it into his
waistband, and strutted about as big as a major gineral
Your mother begun to pick up her crums immediately,
and has been growing fat ever since. And Nabby run
about from house to house like a crazy bed-bug, telling
'em Jack was alive and was agoing to build up Downingville and make something of it yet.

We got your last letter and the President's Proclamation both together, though I see your letter was written two days first. That proclamation is a capital
thing. You know I've made politics my study for forty years, and I must say it's the most ginuin republican
thing I ever come acrost. But what was most provoking about it, was, all the old federalists in town
undertook to praise it tu. Squire Dudley, you know,
was always a federalist, and an Adams man tu. I met
him the next day after the Proclamation come, and he
was chock full of the matter. Says he, Mr. Downing,
that Proclamation is jest the thing. It's the true constitutional doctrine. We all support the President in
this business through thick and thin.

My dander began to rise, and I could n't hold in any
longer. Says I squire Dudley shut up your clack, or
I'll knock your clam-shells together pretty quick' It's
got to be a pretty time of day indeed, if, after we've
worked so hard, to get President Jackson in, you Federalists are going to undertake to praise his proclamation, as much as though he was your own President.—

You've a right to grumble and find fault with it as much as you like; but dont let me hear you say another word in favor of it, if you do I'll make daylight shine through you. The old man hauled in his horns and marched off looking shamed enough.

The next day we concluded to have a public meeting to pass resolutions in favor of the Proclamation. *I* was appointed chairman. The federal party all come flocking round and wanted to come in and help praise the President. We told 'em no; it was our President, and our Proclamation, and they must keep their distance. So we shut the doors and went on with our resolutions. By and by the Federal party began to hurra for Jackson outside the house. At that I told Sargent Joel and your cousin Ephraim and two or three more of the young democrats to go out and clear the coast of them are fellers. And they went out and Sargent Joel drew his piece of a scythe and went at 'em and the Federalists run like a flock of sheep with a dog after 'em. So we finished our resolutions without getting a drop of federalism mixed with 'em, and sent 'em on to the President by Sargent Joel. He got his company together last week, and they filled their knapsacks with bread and sasages and doe-nuts, and started for Washington according to your orders.

I was glad to see that hint in your letter about a post office here. We need one very much. And if the President should think I ought to have it, being I've always been such a good friend to him, why you know, Jack, I'm always ready to serve my country.

So I remain your loving uncle,

JOSHUA DOWNING.

P.S. If the President should n't say any thing more about the post office, I think you had better name it to him again before you go to South Carolina; for if any thing shonld happen to you there, he might never do any more about it.

LETTER XLII.

*Sargent Joel with his company arrives at Washington.
His account of Gen. Blair's fraca with Duff Green.*

Washington City, Jan. 4, 1833.

To my dear Cousin Ephraim Downing, what watches the
Legislater, at Augusta, away down east, in the State of
Maine, while I stay here and look arter Congress and the
President.

DEAR COUSIN,—Sargent Joel got here day before
yesterday, with my hearty old company of Downiug-
ville boys, that went down to Madawaska with me last
winter. They cut rather a curious figure marching
through Pennsylvany Avenu. One half of 'em had
worn their shoes out so that their toes stuck out like the
heads of so many young turkles, and t'other half had
holes through their knees or elbows, and Sargent Joel
marched ahead of 'em swinging his piece of an old
scythe for a sword, and inquiring of every one he met
for Major Jack Downing. They all told him to keep
along till he got to the President's house, which was
the biggest house in the city except the Congress house,
and there he would find me. I and the President were
setting by the window in the great east room, looking
out, and talking about Mr. Calhoun and so on, when
the President began to stare as though he saw a catamount.

He started upon his feet, and says he, Major Downing, if my eyes dont deceive me there's Nullification
now coming up Pennsylvany Avenu. He begun to call
for his pistols, and to tell his men to fasten up the doors
when I looked out, and I knew Joel's strut in a minit.
Says I, dear Gineral that's no nullification, but it's
what'll put a stopper on nullification pretty quick if it
once gets to South Carolina. It's my Downingville

Company commanded by Sargent Joe!. At that the
President looked more pleased than I've seen him before since he got the news of the vote of Pennsylvany.
He ordered 'em into the east room, and gave 'em as
much as they could eat and drink of the best the house
affords. He has found quarters for 'em in the neigh-
bourhood, and says we must be ready to march for South
Carolina whenever he says the word.

But I'll tell you what 't is, cousin Ephraim, I begin
to grow a little kind of wamble cropt about going to
South Carolina, arter all. If they've got many such
fellers there as one Gineral Blair there is here from
that State, I'd sooner take my chance in the woods
forty miles above Downingville, fighting bears and
wolves and catamounts, than come within gun-shot of
one of these Carolina giants. He's a whaler of a feller,
as big as any two men in Downingville. They say he
weighs over three hundred pounds. About a week
ago he met Gineral Duff Green in the street and he
fell afoul of him with a great club and knocked him
down, and broke his arm and beat him almost to death
jest because he got mad at something Mr. Green said
in his paper. And what makes me feel more skittish
about getting into the hands of such chaps, is, because
he says he couldn't help it. He says all his friends
persuaded him not to meddle with Gineral Green, and
he tried as hard as he could to let him alone, but he
' found himself unequal to the effort.' So Green like to
got killed.

The folks here sot out to carry him to court bout it,
but he said he wouldn't go, and so he armed himself
with four pistols and two dirks and a great knife, and
said he'd shoot the first man that touched him. Last
night he went to the Theatre with all his arms and cou-
trements about him. And after he sot there a spell,
and all the folks were looking to see the play go on, he
draws out one of his pistols and fires it at the players.
Then there was a dreadful uproar. They told him he
must clear out about the quickest. But he said if

they'd let him alone he 'd behave like a gentleman. So they went on with the play again.

By and by he draws out another pistol and points it towards the players. At that there was a whole parcel of 'em seized him and dragged him out into another room, big as he was. But pretty soon he got upon his feet, and begun to rave like a mad ox. He pulled off his coat and threw it down, and declared he 'd fight the whole boodle of 'em. The constables were all so frightened they cut and run, and nobody dared to go a near him, till he got cooled down a little, when some of his friends coaxed him away to a tavern. Now as for going to South Carolina to fight such chaps as these, I'd sooner let nullification go to grass and eat mullen.

Sargent Joel told me when he left Downingville you had jest got loaded up with apples and one thing another to go down to Augusta to peddle 'em out; and that you was a going to stay there while the Legislater folks were there. So I thought it would be a good plan for you and I to write to one another about once a week or so, how matters get along.

Give my love to the folks up in Downingville whenever you see 'em.

So I remain your loving Cousin,

MAJOR JACK DOWNING.

LETTER XLIII.

The Major's opinion about Nullification, and his singular illustration of it.

Washington City, Jan. 17, 1833.

To the editor of the Portland Courier, in the Mariners' Church Building, second story, eastern end, Fore street, away down east in State of Maine.

MY KIND AND DEAR OLD FRIEND,—The President's Message to Congress makes cracking work here. Mr. Calhoun shows his teeth like a lion. Mr. McDuffie is cool as a cowcumber, though they say he's got a terrible tempest inside of him, that he 'll let out before long. For my part I think the President's Message is about right. I was setting with the President in the east room last night, chatting about one thing and another, and the President says he, Major Downing, have you read my message that I sent to Congress to day. I told him I had n't. Well, says he, I should like to have you read it and give me your opinion upon it. So he handed it to me and I sot down and read it through.

And when I got through, now says I Gineral I'll tell you jest what I think of this ere business. When I was a youngster some of us Downingville boys used to go down to Sebago Pond every spring and hire out a month or two rafting logs across the Pond. And one time I and cousin Ephraim, and Joel, and Bill Johnson, and two or three more of us had each a whapping great log to carry across the Pond. It was rather a windy day and the waves kept the logs bobbing up and down pretty considerable bad, so we agreed to bring 'em along side and side and lash 'em together and drive some thole-pins in the outermost logs and row 'em over together. We went along two or three miles pretty well. But by and by Bill Johnson begun to complain. He was always an

K

uneasy harumscarum sort of a chap. Always thought
every body else had an easier time than he had, and
when he was a boy, always used to be complaining that
the other boys had more butter on their bread than he
had. Well, Bill was rowing on the leward side, and he
begun to fret and said his side went the hardest, and
he would n't give us any peace till one of us changed
sides with him.

Well Bill had n't rowed but a little ways on the wind-
ward side before he began to fret again, and declared
that side went harder than 'tother, and he would n't
touch to row on that side any longer. We told him he
had his choice, and he should n't keep changing so. But
he only fretted the more and begun to get mad. At last
he declared if we didn't change with him in five minutes,
he'd cut the lashings and take his log and paddle off
alone. And before we had hardly time to turn round,
he declared the five minutes were out, and up hatchet
and cut the lashiugs, and away went Bill on his own log,
bobbing and rolling about, and dancing like a monkey to
try to keep on the upper side. The rest of us scrabbled
to as well as we could, and fastened our logs together
again, though we had a tuff match for it, the wind blew
so hard. Bill had n't gone but a little ways before his
log begun to role more and more, and by and by in he
went splash, head and ears. He came up puffing and
blowing, and got hold of the log and tried to climb up on
to it, but the more he tried the more the log rolled; and
finding it would be gone goose with him pretty soon if
he staid there, he begun to sing out like a loon for us to
come and take him. We asked him which side he would
row if we would take his log into the raft again. O,
says Bill, I'll row on either side or both sides if you
want me to, if you'll only come and help me before I
sink.

But, said the President, I hope you did n't help the
foolish rascal out till he got a pretty good soaking. He
got soaked enough before we got to him, says I, for he
was jest ready to sink for the last time, and our logs

come pesky near getting scattered, and if they had, we should all gone to the bottom together. And now Gineral, this is jest what I think: if you let South Carolina cut the lashings you'll see such a log-rolling in this country as you never see yet. The old Gineral started up and marched across the floor like a boy. Says he, Major Downing, she sha'nt cut the lashings while my name is Andrew Jackson. Tell Sargent Joel to have his company sleep on their arms every night. I told him they should be ready at a moment's warning.

I wish you would jest give cousin Ephraim up to Augusta a jog to know why he dont write to me and let me know how the Legislater is getting along.

I remain your loving friend,
MAJOR JACK DOWNING.

LETTER XLIV.

Major Downing's account of political promises, and their peculiar value.

Augusta, State of Maine, Jan. 30, 1833.

To the Editor of the Portland Courier, that we take up in Downingville; dear sir, I want you to send this on to cousin Jack to Washington City, 'cause he told me you would send it and not charge any postage.

To Major Jack Downing.

DEAR COUSIN JACK,—I got your letter some time ago, but I had n't time to answer it afore now, because I had to go back up to Downingville to get another load of apples. These Legislater folks cronch apples down by the wholesale between speeches, and sometimes in the

middle of speeches tu.   That arternoon that Mr. Clark
spoke all day, I guess I sold nigh upon a half a bushel
for cash, and trusted out most three pecks besides.   The
folks up to Downingville are all pretty well, only your
poor old mother; she's got the reumatics pretty bad
this winter.   She says she wishes with all her heart
Jack would come home, and not think of going to South
Carolina.   Ever since she heard about Gineral Blair
she cant hardly sleep nights, she's so afraid you'll get
shot.   I tell her there's no danger of you as long as
you have President Jackson one side of you and Ser-
gent Joel 'tother.

The Legislater is jogging along here pretty well; I
guess they'll get through about the first of March, if
they dont have too many boundary questions come
along.   We made some Major Ginerals here 'tother
day, and I tried to get you elected.   Not because I
thought you cared much about the office now. but jest
for the honor of Downingville.   I tried most all the
members, and thought to be sure you would come in as
slick as greese.   For about forty of 'em told me they
thought it belonged to you.   They said it was against
their principles to pledge their votes to any body; but
they whispered in my ear that they would *do what they
could,* and they had n't *scarčely* a doubt but what you'd
be elected.   Sixty eight of 'em told me you was the
best man for it, and would undoubtedly be chosen as a
matter of course.   And twentyfive, of 'em promised me
right up and down by the crook of the elbow, that they
would vote for you.

Well Jack, after all this, you did n't get but *two
vote* by that time I begun to think it was n't so strange
that it took two years heard fishimg before you could
get an office.

This is the most democratic Legislater that they have
ever had in this state yet.   They are most all real ginuin democrats, and they give Mr Holmes and Mr
Sprague a terrible basting for being federlists, and they
have turned Mr Holmes out and put Mr. Shepley in.

The Legislater is talking of moving the seat of government back to Portland again. They say it will be better all round. They wont have to go so fur through the snow-drifts to their boarding houses, and wont have to pay much more than half so much for their board.— And here they have to pay four pence apiece every time they are shaved; but in Portland they can get shaved by the half dozen for three cents apiece. I hope they will go, for I can get more for my apples in Portland than I can here.

P. S. Bill Johnson was married last week, and he quarrelled with his wife the very next day. So you see he is the same old sixpence he used to be. He says he 'll send a petition to the Legislater to be divorced, and he declares if they dont't grant it, he 'll cut the lashings as he did once on the raft on Sebago Pond, sink or swim.

N. B. Uncle Joshua wished me to ask you to ask the President about that post office again, as his commission has n't come yet.

I remain your loving Cousin,

EPHRAIM DOWNING.

K 2

LETTER XLV.

*The Major ascends to the top of Congress house and
listens to see if he can hear the guns in South Carolina—he converses with the president about the newspaper slanders.*

Washington City, Feb. 1, 1833.

To the editor of the Portland Courier, in Mariners' Church
Building, second story, eastern end, Fore Street away down
east, in the State of Maine.

MY DEAR FRIEND.—This is nullification day, and
it's most night, and I aint dead yet, and hant been
shot at once to-day. I got up this morning as soon as
it was light, and went out and looked away towards
South Carolina, and listened as hard as I could to see
if I could hear the guns crackin and the cannons roarin.
But it was all still as a mouse. And I've been up top
the Congress house five or six times to-day and listened and listened, but all the firing I could hear was inside the Congress house itself, where the members
were shooting their speeches at each other. I had my
company all ready this morning with their dinners in
their napsacks, to start as quick as we heard a single
gun. We shant go till we hear something from these
nullifiers, for the president says he aint agoing to begin
the scrape, but if the nullifiers begin it, then the hardest must fend off.

Yesterday a friend handed me a couple of papers
printed at Hallowell away down pretty near to Augusta in the state of Maine, called the American Advo-
cate, and I found something in 'em that made me as
mad as March hair. The first one mentioned that Capt.
Dow was chosen mayor of Portland, and then said, he
is the reputed author of the Jack Downing letters that
have been published in the Portland Courier. The
other paper that was printed two or three days after-

wards, said Mr. Dow the mayor of Portland is not the author of Jack Downing's letters ; they are written by Mr. Seba Smith, the Editor of the Portland Courier. Now, Mr. Editor, my good old friend, is n't this too bad? I have n't come acrost any thing that made me feel so wamblecropt this good while. Jest as if Major Jack Downing could n't write his own letters.

I've been to school, put it altogether, off and on, more than six months , and though I say it myself, I always used to be called the best scholar among the boys in Downingville, and most always used to stand at the head of my class. I'd been through Webster's spelling-book before I was fifteen, and before I was twenty I could cypher to the rule of three. And now to have it said that I dont write my own letters, is too bad. It's what I call a rascally shame. I was so boiling over with it last night, that I could n't hold in ; and so I took the papers and went in and showed them to the president. I always go to the president when I have any difficulty, and when he has any he comes to me ; so we help one another along as well as we can. When the president had read it, says he, Major Downing, it's strange to see how this world is given to lying. The pnblic papers are beginning to slander you jest as they always do me. I have n't written scarcely a public document since I've been president, but what it's been laid off to Mr. Van Buren, or Mr. McLane, or Mr. Livingston, or Mr. Taney, or somebody or other. And how to help this slanderous business I dont know. But it's too provoking, Major, that's certain. Sometimes I've a good mind to make Congress pass a law that every editor who says I dont write my proclamations and messages, or that you dont write your letters, shall forfeit his press and types ; and if that dont stop him, that he shall be strung up by the neck without judge or jury.

And now, Mr. Editor, I wish you would jest give that Hallowell man a hint to mind his own p's and q's in future, and look out for his neck. And as you

know very well that I do write my own letters, I
would thank you jest to tell the public so.
   I remain your sincere and loving friend,
           MAJOR JACK DOWNING

LETTER XLVI.

*Cousin Ephraim explains the science of land specula-
tion.*

Augusta, State of Maine, March, 4, 1833.

*To Major jack Downing, at President Jackson's house
in Washington City.*

DEAR COUSIN JACK,—The Legislater folks have all
cleared out to-day one arter t'other jest like a flock of
sheep; and some of 'em have left me in the lurch tu, for
they cleared out without paying me for my apples.
Some of 'em went off in my debt as much as twenty
cents, and some ninepence, and a shilling, and so on.
They all kept telling me when they got paid off, they'd
settle up with me.   And so I waited with patience till
they adjourned, and thought I was as sure of my money
as though it was in the Bank.
   But, my patience, when they did adjourn, such a hubbub I guess you never see.   They were flying about
from one room to another, like so many pigeons shot in
the head.   They run into Mr. Harris' room and clawed
the money off of his table, hand over fist.   I brustled up
to some of 'em, and tried to settle.   I come to one man
that owed me twelve cents, and he had a ninepence in
change, but he would n't let me have that, because he
should lose a half cent.   So, while we were bothering
about it, trying to get it changed, the first I knew the
rest of 'em had got their money in their pockets and
were off like a shot, some of 'em in stages, and some in

sleighs, and some footing it. I out and followed after em, but 'twas no use; I could n't catch one of 'em. And as for my money, and apples tu, I guess I shall have to whistle for 'em now. Its pesky hard, for I owe four and sixpence here yet for my board, and I've paid away every cent I 've got for my apples, and dont know but I shall have to come down with another load to clear out my expenses. Howsomever, you know uncle Joshua always told us never to cry for spilt milk, so I mean to hold my head up yet.

I dont know but I shall have to give up retailing apples, I meet with so many head-flaws about it. I was thinking that, soon as the Legislater adjourned, I'd take a load of apples and apple-sass, and a few sassages, and come on to Washington, and go long with your company to South Carolina. But they say Mr. Clay has put a stopper on that nullification business, so that its ten chances to one you wont have to go.

I dont care so much about the apple business after all; for I've found out a way to get rich forty times as fast as I can by retailing apples, or as you can by hunting after an office. And I advise you to come right home, as quick as you can come. Here's a business going on here that you can get rich by, ten times as quick as you can in any office, even if you should get to be President. The President dont have but twenty-five thousand dollars a year; but in this ere business that's goin on here, a man can make twenty-five thousand dollars in a week if he's a mind to, and not work hard neither.

I spose by this time you begin to feel rather in a pucker to know what this business is. I 'll tell you: but you must keep it to yourself, for if all them are Washington folks and Congress folks should come on here and go to dipping into it, I'm afraid they'd cut us all out. But between you and me, its only jest buying and selling land. Why, Jack, its forty times more profitable than money digging, or any other business that you ever see. I knew a man here t'other day from Bangor, that made ten thousand dollars, and I guess he want more than an hour about it. Most all the folks here and down to Portland and Bangor have got their fortunes made, and now we are beginning to take hold of it up in the country.

They 've got a slice up in Downingville, and I missed it by being down here selling apples, or I should had a finger in the pie. Uncle Joshua Downing, you know he's an old fox, and always knows where to jump; well, he see how every body was getting rich, so he went and bought a piece of a township up back of Downingville, and give his note for a thousand dollars for it. And then he sold it to uncle Jacob and took his note for two thousand dollars; and uncle Jacob sold it to uncle Zackary and took his note for three thousand dollars; and uncle Zackary sold it to uncle Jim, and took his note for four thousand dollars; and uncke Jim sold it to cousin Sam, and took his note for five thousand dollars; and cousin Sam sold it to Bill Johnson, and took his note for six thousand dollars. So you see there's five of 'em that want worth ninepence apiece before, have now got a thousand dollars apiece clear, when their notes are paid. And Bill Johnson's going to logging off of it, and they say he 'll make more than any of 'em.

Come home, Jack, come home by all means, if you want to get rich. Give up your commission, and think no more about being President, or any thing else, but come home and buy land before its all gone.

Your loving Cousin,
EPHRAIM DOWNING.

P. S. Did n't Mr. Holmes and Mr. Sprague look rather blue when they got the resolutions that our Legislater passed, giving them such a mortal whipping?

LETTER XLVII.

Major Downing's account of the manner in which Mr. Clay put a stop to the fuss in South Carolina, and his pacification bill to hush up the quarrels of the nullifiers.

Washington City, March 10, 1833.

To the editor of the Portland Courier, in the Mariners' Church building, 2nd story, eastern end, Fore Street, away down east, in the State of Maine, to be sent to Cousin Ephraim Downing, up in Downingville, cause I spose he's gone home before this time from Augusta.

DEAR COUSIN EPHRAIM,—I got your letter this morning. It was a shame for them are Legislater folks to skulk off without paying you for your apples. But they are the worst folks about standing to their word that I know of. They 've promised me an office more than twenty times, but some how or other, come to the case in hand, their votes always went for somebody else. But I dont care a fig for 'em as long as I 've got the President on my side, for his offices are as fat again as the Legislater offices are. The President's offices will support a man pretty well if he does 'nt do any thing at all. As soon as Mr. Clay's Tariff Bill passed, the President called me into his room, and says he, Major Downing, the nullification jig is up. There'll be no fun for you in South Carolina now, and I guess you may as well let Sargent Joel march the company back to Downingville, and wait till somebody kicks up another bobbery some where and then I' ll send for 'em, for they are the likeliest company I 've seen since I went with my Tennessee rangers to New Orleans. And as for you Major Downing, you shall still hold your commission and be under half pay, holding yourself in readiness to march at a moment's warning and to fight whenever called for.

So you see, Cousin Ephraim, I am pretty well to live in the world, without any of your land speculations or

apple selling down east.   I cant seem to see how 'tis
they all make money so fast in that land business down
there that you tell about.   How could all our folks and
Bill Johnson and all of 'em there in Downingville make
a thousand dollars a piece, jest a trading round among
themselves, when there aint fifty dollars in money, put
it all together. in the whole town.   It rather puzzles
me a little.   As soon as I see 'em all get their thousand
dollars cash in hand, I guess I 'll give up my commission and come home and buy some land tu.

But at present I think I rather have a bird in the
hand than one in the bush.   Our Congress folks here
cleared out about the same time that your Legislater
folks did, and I and the President have been rather
lonesome a few days.   The old gentleman says I
must n't leave him on any account ; but I guess I shall
start Joel and the company off for Downingville in a
day or two.   They 've got their clothes pretty much
mended up, and they look quite tidy.   I should n't feel
ashamed to see'em marched through any city in the
United States.

It is n't likely I shall have any thing to do under my
commission very soon.   For some say there 'll be no
more fighting in the country while Mr. Clay lives, if
it should be a thousand years.   He's got a master knack
of pacifying folks and hushing up quarrels as you ever
see.   He's stopt all that fuss in South Carolina, that you
know was jest ready to blow the whole country sky
high.   He stept to 'em in Congress and told 'em what
sort of a Bill to pass, and they passed it without hardly
any jaw about it.   And South Carolina has hauled in
her horns, and they say she'll be as calm as a clock
now.   And that is n't the only quarrel Mr. Clay has
stopt.   Two of the Senators, Mr. Webster and Mr.
Poindexter. got as mad as March hairs at each other.
They called each other some pesky hard names, and
looked cross enough for a week to bite a board nail off.
Well, after Mr. Clay got through with South Carolina,
he took them in hand.   He jest talked to 'em about five

minutes, and they got up and went and shook hands with each other, and looked as loving as two brothers.

Then Mr. Holmes got up and went to Mr. Clay, and almost with tears in his eyes asked him if he would n't be so kind as to settle a little difficulty there was between him and his constituents, so they might elect him to Congress again. And I believe some of the other Senators asked for the same favor.

So as there is likely to be peace now all round the house for some time to come, I'm in a kind of a quandary what course to steer this summer. The President talks of taking a journey down east this summer, and he wants me to go with him, because I 'm acquainted there, and can show him all about it. He has a great desire to go as fur as Downingville, and get acquainted with Uncle Joshua, who has always stuck by him in all weathers through thick and thin. The President thinks uncle Joshua is one of the republican pillars of New England, and says he shall always have the post office as long as he lives, and his children after him.

I rather guess on the whole I shall come on that way this summer with the President. But wherever I go, I shall remain your loving cousin,

MAJOR JACK DOWNING.

LETTER XLVIII.

The Major's account of the consultation amongst the government on the question, whether the President shakes hands with the federalists, during his journey down East.

Washington City, April 20, 1833.

To the Editor of the Portland Courier, in the Mariners' Church building, second story, eastern end, Fore Street, away down east, in the State of Maine.

MY DEAR OLD FRIEND, — Bein I hant writ to you for some time, I'm afraid you and our folks up in Downingville will begin to feel a little uneasy by and by, so I'll jest write you a little if it aint but two lines, to let you know how we get on here. I and the President seem to enjoy ourselves pretty well together, though its getting to be a little lonesome since the Congress folks went off, and Sargent Joel cleared out with my Downingville Company, Poor souls, I wonder if they have got home yet; I have n't heard a word from 'em since they left here. I wish you would send up word to Sargeant Joel to write to me and let me know how they got along. He can send his letter in your Currier, or get uncle Joshua to frank it; either way it wont cost me any thing. Now I think of it, I wish you would jest ask cousin Nabby to ask uncle Joshua to frank me on two or three pair of stockings, for mine have got terribly out at the heels. He can do it jest as well as not; they make nothing here of franking a bushel basket full of great books to the western States. And they say some of the members of Congress used to frank their clothes home by mail to be washed.

I and the President are getting ready to come on that way this summer. We shall come as far as Portland, and I expect we shall go up to Downingville; for the President says he must shake hands with uncle Joshua before he comes back, that faithful old republican who has stood by him through thick and thin ever since he found he was going to be elected President. He will either go up to Downingville, or send for Uncle Joshua to meet him at Portland.

There is some trouble amongst us here a little, to know how we shall get along among the federalists when we come that way. They say the federalists in Massachusetts want to keep the President all to themselves when he comes there. But Mr. Van Buren says that 'll never do; he must stick to the democratic party: he may shake hands with a federalist once in a while if the democrats dont see him, but whenever there 's any democrats round he must n't look at a federalist. Mr. McLane and Mr. Livingston advise him tother way.—

They tell him he'd better treat the federalists pretty civil, and shake hands with Mr. Webster as quick as he would with uncle Joshua Downing. And when they give this advice Mr. Lewis and Mr. Kendle hop right up as mad as march hairs, and tell him if he shakes hands with a single federalist while he is gone, the democratic party will be ruined. And then the President turns to me and asks me what he had better do. And I tell him I guess he better go straight ahead, and keep a stiff upper lip, and shake hands with whoever he is a mind to.

Mr. Van Buren staid with us awhile at the President's, but he's moved into a house now on Pennsylvany Avenue. He's a fine slick man I can tell you, and the President says he's the greatest man in America. He's got the beat'em-est tongue that I ever see. If you had a black hat on, he could go to talking to you and in ten minutes he could make you think it was white.

Give my love to our folks up in Downingville when you have a chance to send it to 'em, and believe me your old friend,

MAJOR JACK DOWNING.

LETTER XLIX.

Major Downing defends the President against the assaults of Lieut. Randolph, on board the Cygnet steam boat.

On board the steam-boat Cygnet, near the city of Alexandria, down a little ways below Washington, May the 6th, 1833.

To the Editor of the Portland Courier in the Mariners' church Building, 2nd story, Eastern end, Fore street, away down East, in the State of Maine.

MY DEAR OLD FRIEND.—We 've had a kind of a hurly burly time here to-day. I did n't know but we

should burst the biler one spell ; and some of us, as
it was, got scalding hot. You see, I and the president and a few more gentlemen got into the steam-
boat this morning to go round into old Virginny to
help lay the foundation of a monument, so they should
n't forget who Washington's mother was.

When we got down along to Alexandria, the boat
hauled up to the side of the wharf awhile to let some
more folks get in, and while she lay there, I and the
president and a few more of 'em sot in the cabin reading and chatting with one another. The president
had jest got through reading a letter from uncle
Joshua Downing, urging him very strongly to come
up as fur as Downingville when he comes on that way.
And says he, Major Downing, this uncle Joshua of
yours is a real true blue republican as I know of any
where. I would n't miss seeing him when I go down
east for a whole year's salary.

Says I, your honor, Downingville is the most thorough
going republican town there is any where in the eastern country ; and you ought not to come back till
you have visited it.   Jest as I said that there was a
stranger came into the cabin and stept along up to the
president, and begun to pull off his glove. I thought
there was some mischief bruing, for his lips were kind
of quivery, and I did n't like the looks of his eyes
a bit.   But the president thought he was trying to
get his gloves off to shake hands with him, and the
good old man is always ready to shake hands with a
friend ; so he reached out his hand to him and smiled,
and told him never to stand for the gloves, and the
words want hardly out of his mouth when dab went one
of the fellow's hands slap into the president's face.

In a moment I levelled my umbrella at the villain's
head, and came pesky near fetching him to the floor.
Two more gentlemen then clenched him by the collar
and had him down as quick as ever you see a beef ox
knocked down with an ax. In a minute there was a
crowd round him as thick as a swarm of bees,

But, my stars, I wish you could have seen the president jest at that minute. If you ever see a lioh lying down asleep and a man come along with a great club and hit him a plot with all his might, and then see that lion spring on his feet, and see the fire flash in his eyes, and hear him roar and gnash his teeth, you might give some sort of a guess what kind of a harrycane we had of it.

The old Gineral no sooner felt the fellow's paw in his face than he sprung like a steel-trap, and catched his cane and went at him. But there was such a crowd of men there in an instant, that it was as much impossible to get through 'em as it was for the British to get through his pile of cotton wool bags at New-Orleans. If it had n't been for that, I dont think but he would have kicked the feller through the side of the steamboat in two minutes.

However, somehow or other the rascal got hussled out of the boat on to the wharf, and fled like a dog that had been stealing sheep. They have sent some officers after him, but where they will overtake him nobody knows.

The president has got cleverly cooled down again, and we are going on to lay the foundation of the monument.

My love to all the good folks up in Downingville.

In haste your old friend,

MAJOR JACK DOWNING.

LETTER L.

Major Downing tells how he shook hands for the President while at Philadelphla. on his tour down East.

To Uncle Joshua Downing, Post Master, up in Downingville, in the State of Maine. This to be sent by my old friend, the Editor of the Portland Courier, with care and speed.

Philadelphia, June 10, 1833.

DEAR UNCLE JOSHUA,—We are coming on full chisel. I've been trying, ever since we started, to

L 2

get a chance to write a little to you; but when we've been on the road I couldn't catch my breath hardly long enough to write my name, we kept flying so fast; and when we made any stop, there was such a jam round us there wasn't elbow room enough for a miskeeter to turn round without knocking his wings off.

I'm most afraid now we shall get to Downingville before this letter does, so that we shall be likely to catch you all in the suds before you think of it. But I understand there is a *fast mail* goes on that way, and I mean to send it by that, so I'm in hopes you'll get it time enough to have the children's faces washed and their heads combed, and the gals get on their clean grwns. And if Sargent Joel *could* have time enough to call out my old Downingville Company and get their uniform brushed up a little, and come down the road as fur as your new barn to meet us, there's nothing that would please the President better. As for victuals, most any thing wont come amiss; we are as hungry as bears after travelling a hundred miles a day. A little fried pork and eggs, or a pot of baked beans and an Indian pudding would suit us much better than the soft stuff they give us here in these great cities.

The President wouldn't miss of seeing you for any thing in the world, and he will go to Downingville if he has legs and arms enough left when he goes to Portland to carry him there. But for fear any thing should happen that he shouldn't be able to come, you had better meet us in Portland, say about the 22d, and then you can go up to Downingville with us, you know.

This travelling with the President is capital fun after all, if it wasn't so plaguy tiresome. We come into Baltimore on a Rail Road, and we flew over the ground like a harrycane. There isn't a horse in this country that could keep up with us, if he should go upon the clean clip. When we got to Baltimore, the streets were filled with folks as thick as the spruce trees down in your swamp. There we found Black Hawk, a little, old, dried up Indian king. And I thought the folks looked at him and the prophet about as much as they did me and the President. I gave the President a wink that this Indian fellow was taking the shine off of us a little, so we concluded we wouldn't have him in our company any more, and shall git on without him.

I cant stop to tell you in this letter how we got along to Philadelphy, though we had a pretty easy time some of the way in the steam-boats. And I cant stop to tell you of half of the fine things I have seen here. They took us up into a great hall this morning as big as a meeting-house, and then the folks begun to pour in by thousands to shake hands with the President; federalists and all, it made no difference. There was such a stream of 'em coming in that the hall was full in a few minutes, and it was so jammed up round the door that they couldn't get out again if they were to die. So they had to knock out some of the windows and go out tother way.

The President shook hands with all his might an hour or two, till he got so tired he couldn't hardly stand it. I took hold and shook for him once in awhile to help him along, but at last he got so tired he had to lay down on a soft bench covered with cloth and shake as well as he could, and when he couldn't shake he'd nod to 'em as they come along. And at last he got so beat out, he couldn't only wrinkle his forhead and wink. Then I kind of stood behind him and reached my arm round under his, and shook for him for about a half an hour as tight as I could spring. Then we concluded it was best to adjourn for to-day.

And I've made out to get away up into the garret in the tavern long enough to write this letter. We shall be off to-morrow or next day for York, and if I can possibly get breathing time enough there, I shall write to you again.

Give my love to all the folks in Downingville, and believe me your loving neffu,

MAJOR JACK DOWNING.

LETTER LI.

Major Downing and the President's narrow escape at the breaking down of the bridge extending from Castle Garden to the Battery at New York.

To uncle Joshua Downing, Post Master up in Downingville, State of Maine, to be sent in the Portland Courier with care and speed.

New York City, Friday evening, June 14, 1833.

Dear Uncle Joshua,—Here we are amongst an ocean of folks, and cutting up capers as high as a cat's back. I spose you will see by the papers how we all like to got drowned yesterday going acros a little bridge between the castle and the garden.

It was a pesky narrow squeak for me and the President. He was riding over on a great fine hoss, and I was walking along by the side of him and trying to clear the way a little, for they crowded upon us so, there was no getting along, and hardly a chance to breathe. When we got under the arch we stopped a little bit for the crowd to clear away, when all at once I thought I heard something crack. Says I, Gineral you better go ahead, I'm afraid there's mischief bruing here. At that he give his hoss a lick and pushed through the crowd, but we had n't got more than a rod, before crash went the bridge behind us, all down in a heap, and two toll-houses on top of it and as many as a hundred folks splashed into tne water, all mixed up together one top of 'tother. The President looked over his shoulder, and seeing I was safe behind him, called out for Mr. Van Buren, and asked me to run and see if he was hurt. I told him he had forgot himself, for Mr. Van Buren was n't in the company; but Mr. Woodbury and Mr. Cass were in for it, for I could see them floundering about in the water now. Run, Major, said the President run and give them a lift. Take Mr. Woodbury first, you know I can't spare him at any rate.

So there was a parcel of us took hold and went to hauling of 'em out of the water like so many drownded rats. But we got 'em all out alive, except a few young things they called dandies; they looked so after they got wet all over that we could n't make out whether they were alive or dead. So we laid 'em up to dry and left 'em; and I went on to help the President review the troops on the battery, as they call it; and a grand place it is tu. I 've seen more fine shows here, it seems to me, than ever I see before in my life. Such a sight of folks, and fine ladies, and fine houses, and vessels, and steamboats, and flags a flying, and cannons firing, and fire works a whisking about, I never see the beat of it. I did n't think there was so much fun in this world before, for all I've been about so much at Madawaska and among the nullifiers and all round.

But I cant tell you much about it till we get there, for I cant find any time to write. I've only cheated a few minutes this evening while the President is gone into Mr. Niblo's garden. One of the master sights that I've seen yet was that baloon that went up this afternoon, carrying a man with it. Poor fellow, I dont much think he 'll ever get back again, for he looked to me the last I see of him as though he would land in England, or the moon, or some other country.

All these sights keep us back a little longer than we expected. I dont think now we shall be in Portland before the 28th or 29th of this month. So I thought I'd jest write you a line that you might be down there about that time.

In haste your loving neffu,
MAJOR JACK DOWNING

LETTER LII.

Visit of Major Jack Downing and the President to Boston—the rascally conduct of the letter writer in his name for the newspapers.

Boston, Tuesday, June 25, 1833.

To the Editor of the Portland Courier.

MY DEAR OLD FRIEND,—I 'm keeping house with the President to-day, and bein he's getting considerable better, I thought I'd catch a chance when he was taking a knap, and write a little to let you know how we get along. This ere sickness* of the President has been a bad pull-back to us. He hasn't been able to go out since Sunday afternoon, and I've been watchin with him this two nights, and if I wasn't as tough as a halter, I should be half dead by this time.

And if the President want tougher than a catamount, he'd kick the bucket before he'd been round to see one half the notions there is in Boston. Poor man, he has a hard time of it; you've no idea how much he has to go through. Its worse than being dragged through forty knot holes.

To be bamboozled about from four o'clock in the morning till midnight, rain or shine, jammed into one great house to eat a breakfast, and into another great house to eat a dinner, and into another to eat supper, and into two or three others between meals, to eat cooliations, and to have to go out and review three or four rigiments of troops, and then to be jammed into Funnel Hall two hours, and shake hands with three or four thousand folks, and then to go into the State House and stand there two or thee hours and see all Boston streaming through it like a river through a sawmill, and then

---

* The President was a few days sick while in Boston.

to ride about the city awhile in a fine painted covered
waggon with four or five horses to draw it, and then ride
awhile in one without any cover to it, finney-fined off to
the top notch, and then get on to the horses and ride
awhile a horseback, and then run into a great picture
room and see more fine pictures than you could shake a
stick at in a week, and then go into some grand gentleman's house, and shake hands a half an hour with a
flock of ladies, and then after supper go and have a little still kind of a hubbub all alone with three or four
hundred particular friends, and talk an hour or two, and
take another cooliation, and then go home, and about
midnight get ready to go to bed, and up again at four
o'clock the next morning and at it.—If this aint enough
to tucker a feller out I dont know what is. The President wouldn't have stood it till this time if he hadn't
sent me and Mr. Van Buren and the rest of us to some
of the parties, while he staid at home to rest.

The President's got so much better I think we shall
be able to start for Salem to-morrow, for we must go
through with it now we've begun, as hard work as 'tis.
I think we shall get to Portland about the 4th of July;
so if you get your guns and things all ready you can
kill two birds with one stone. I hope you'll be pretty
careful there how you point your guns. They pointed
'em so careless at New York that one of the wads come
within six inches of making daylight shine through the
President.

Now I think ont, there is the most rascally set of fellers skulking about somewhere in this part of the country that ever I heard of, and I wish you would blow 'em
up. They are worse than the pick-pockets. I mean
them are fellers that's got to writing letters and putting
my name to 'em, and sending of 'em to the printers.
And I heard there was one sassy feller last Saturday
down to Newburyport that ot on to a horse and rid
about town calling himself Major Jack Downing, and
all the soldiers and the folks marched up and and shook
hands with him, and thought it was me.—Now, my

dear old friend, isn't this too bad? What would you do if you was in my case? I say again they are worse than the pick-pockets. Isn't it Mr. Shakespear that says something about 'he that steals my munny-pus steals trash, but he that steals my name ought to have his head broke?' I wish you would find that story and print it.

There, the President's jest waked up, so I must subscribe myself, in haste, Your friend,

MAJOR JACK DOWNING.

LETTER LIII.

The President orders to the right about face, at Concord, when they beat a march, quick time, back to Washington.

CONCORD, Nu Hamsheer, June 30, 1833.

To the Editor of the Portland Courier.

My DEAR OLD FRIEND,—The jig is all up about our going to Portland and Downingville. I've battled the watch with the President this two days about it, and told him he must go there if he had the breath of life in him; and he kept telling me he certainly would if hoses could carry him there.

But the President is n't very well, and that aint the worst of it; there's been a little difficulty bruin among us, and the President's got so riled about it, that he's finally concluded to start on his way back to-morrow. I cant help it; but I feel bad enough about it. If I wasn't a military man I could cry a barrel of tears.

I dont know how they will stan it in Downingville when they come to get the news. I'm afraid there will be a master uproar there, for you know they are all full-blooded democrats.

But the stage is jest agoing to start, and I've only time to write you this line, in haste from your friend

MAJOR JACK DOWNING.

MAJOR JACK DOWNING'S HOUSE AT DOWNINGVILLE.

M

LETTER LIV.

Major Downings nomination for the Presidency, with an elegant picture of his residence.

NOMINATION FOR THE PRESIDENCY.

From the National Intelligencer.

We do not know whether it be necessary, in copying the subjoined effusion, to enter into a protest against misinterpretation of our motives. We should be sorry to be understood, whilst humouring a jest, as meaning to burlesque so serious an action as the choice of President of the United States. We copy the following for the sake of its moral, as well as its wit, and we do not like the moral the less for being taught with a smiling countenance.

From the Mauch Chunk Courier.

Our next President

Many of the papers in the United States have already manifested a disposition to agitate the subject of the next Presidency, and several distinguished individuals have been informally named for that office, among whom are Mr. Van Buren, Mr. M'Lean, Mr. Cass, Mr. Clay and Mr. Webster. As we are opposed to a premature discussion of this ticklish question, we have not hitherto committed ourself in favour of either of these individuals. Indeed, we have considered it very imprudent in these times, for any one who wishes to be an orthodox politician, to "come out" for any body until he can ascertain who will be most likely to succeed. Accordingly we have stood upon our " reserved rights" of neutrality, to watch the signs of the times, and see who would probably be the most *popular* candidate. Recent indications have satisfactorily convinced us on that point, and as we wish to be considered among the "originals"—the *real Simon Pures*, we would lose no time in nominating

For President,
MAJOR JACK DOWNING,
Of Downingville.

In recommending this distinguished personage to our fellow citizens, it will be scarcely necessary to enumerate his various claims to their suffrages. Suffice it to say, his military renown, his valuable public services in assisting President Jackson to put down the Nullifiers, especially in shaking hands with the Yankees " down east," and last though not least, the fidelity with which he and his uncle Joshua stuck to the Old Hero after he found he was going to be President, eminently qualify him for that exalted station.

LETTER LV.

The Major tells us about the President, being made Doctor of Laws.

On board the Steam-boat, going from Providence to York, July 2, 1833.

To my old friend, the Elitor of the Portland Courier, in the Mariners' Church building, second story, eastern end, Fore Street, away down east, in the state of Maine.

My Dear Friend.—We are driving back again full chisel, as fast as we come on when we were on the Rail Road between Washington and Baltimore. And we've been drivin so fast on a round turn in all the places where we've been, and have had so much shaking hands and eating and one thing another to do, that I could'nt get time to write to you at half the places where I wanted to, so I thought I'd set down now, while the President's laid down to rest him awhile, and tell you something about Cambridge and Lowell. Ye see when we were at Boston they sent word to us

to come out to Cambridge, for they wanted to make
the President a Doctor of Laws.   What upon arth a
Doctor of Laws was, or why they wanted to make the
President one, I could n't think.   So when we come
to go up to bed I asked the Gineral about it.   And says
I, Gineral, what is it they want to do to you out to Cambridge?   Says he they want to make a Doctor of Laws
of me.   Well, says I, but what good will that do?
Why, says he, you know Major Downing, there's a
pesky many of them are laws passed by Congress, that
are rickety things.   Some of 'em have very poor constitutions, and some of 'em have n't no constitutions at
all.   So that it is necessary to have somebody there to
Doctor 'em up a little, and not let 'em go out into the
world where they would stan a chance to catch cold
and be sick, without they had good constitutions to bear
it.   You know, says he, I have had to doctor the Laws
considerable ever since I've been at Washington, although I was n't a regular bred Doctor.   And I made
out so well about it, that these Cambridge folks think I
had better be mad into a regular Doctor at once, and
then there 'll be no grumbling and disputing about my
practice.   Says he, Major, what do you think of it?
I told him I thought it was an excellent plan; and
asked him if he did n't think they would be willing,
bein I'd been round in the military business considerable for a year or two past, to make me a Doctor of War.
He said he did n't know, but he thought it would be
no harm to try 'em.   But says, he Major, I feel a little
kind of streaked about it after all; for they say they
will go talking to me in Latin, and although I studied
it a little once, I dont know any more about it now than
the man in the moon.   And how I can get along in
that case I dont know.   I told him my way, when any
body talked to me in a lingo that I didn't understand,
was jest to say nothing, but look as knowing as any of
'em, and then they thought I knew a pesky sight more
than any of 'em.   At that the Gineral fetched me a
slap on the shoulder and haw hawed right out.   Says

he, Major Downing, you are the boy for me ; I do n't
know how I should get along in this world if it was n't
for you.

So when we got ready we went right to Cambridge
as bold as could be. And that are Cambridge is a real
pretty place; it seems to me I should like to live in
them Colleges as well as any place I've seen. We
went into the Libry, and I guess I stared a little, for I
did n't think before there was half so many books in
the world I should think there was near about enough
to fill a meetin house. I dont believe they was ever
all read or ever will be to all ages.

When we come to go in to be made Doctors of, there
was a terrible crowding round; but they give us a good
place, and then sure enough they did begin to talk in
Latin or some other gibberish; but whether they were
talking to the Gineral, or who 'twas, I could n't tell. I
guess the Gineral was a little puzzled. But he never
said a word, only once in a while bowed a little. And
I spose he happened sometimes to put in the bows in
the wrong place, for I could see some of the sassy stu-
dents look up one side once a while, and snicker out of
one corner of their mouths. Howsomever the Gineral
stood it out like a hero, and got through very well.
And when 'twas over, I stept up to Mr. Quincey and
asked him if he would n't be so good as to make me a
Doctor of War, and hinted to him a little about my
services down to Madawaska and among the nullifiers.
At that he made me a very polite bow, and says he,
Major Downing, we should be very happy to oblige you
if we could, but we never give any degrees of war here;
all our degrees are degrees of peace. So I find I shall
have to practice war in the natural way, let nullification, or what will, come. After 'was all over we went
to Mr. Quincey's and had a capital dinner. And on
the whole had about as good a visit to Cambridge as
most any where.

I meant to a told you considerable about Lowell, but
the steamboat goes so fast, I shant have time to. We

M 2

went all over the Factories; and there ! I wont try to say one word about 'em, for I've been filled with such a wondermient ever since, that my ideas are all as big as hay stacks, and if I should try to get one of 'em out of my head, it would tear it all to pieces. It beat all that ever I heard of before, and the Gineral said it beat all that ever he heard of. But what made the Gineral hold his head up and feel more like a soldier, than he had before since he was at New Orleans, was when we marched along the street by them are five thousand gals, all dressed up and looking as pretty as a million of butterflies. The Gineral marched along as light as a boy, and seems to me I never see his eyes shine so bright afore. After we got along about to the middle of 'em, he whispered to me, and says he, Major Downing, is your Cousin Nabby here among 'em; if she is, I must be introduced to her. I told him she was not; as they were expecting us to come to Downingville, she staid to home to help get ready. Well, says he, if any thing should happen that we can't go to Downingville, you must send for your Cousin Nabby and Uncle Joshua to come on to Washington to see me. I will bear all the expenses, if they will only come, says he; these northern gals are as much afore our southern and western gals as can be, and I've thought of you Cousin Nabby a great deal lately—he looked as though he was going to say something more, but Mr. Van Buren and the rest of 'em crowded up along so near that it broke off, and had to go along.

I see we've got most to York, and shall have to go ashore in a few minutes, so I cant write any more now, but remain your sincere and loving friend,

MAJOR JACK DOWNING.

LETTER LVI.

*An account of the quarrel that the major had with Mr.
Van Buren at Concord, after they went up chamber
to bed, and the declaration of his intentions to run
for the presidency.*

Washington City, July 20, 1833.

To my old friend, the editor of the Portland Courier, away
down east in the state of Maine.

My DEAR OLD FRIEND, YOU.—I dont know but you
might think strange on 't, that I should be back here to
Washington more than a fortnight, and not write to
you. But I hant forgot you. You need n't never be
afraid of that. We aint very apt to forget our best
friends ; and you may depend upon it Jack Downing
will never forget the editor of the Portland Courier any
more than Andrew Jackson will forget Jack Downing.
You was the first person that ever give me a lift into
public life, and you 've been a boosting me along ever
since. And jest between you and me I think I 'm getting into a way now where I shall be able by and by to
do something to pay you for it. The reason that I have
n't writ to you before, is, that we have had pretty serious business to attend to since we got back. But we
've jest got through with it, and Mr. Van Buren has
cleared out and gone back about the quickest to New
York, and I guess with a bed-bug in his ear. Now
jest between you and me in confidence, I'll tell you
how 'tis ; but pray dont let on about it to any body
else for the world. Did n't you think plaguy strange
what made us cut back so quick from Concord without
going to Portland or Portsmouth or Downingville ?
You know the papers have said it was because the president want very well, and the president had to make
that excuse himself in some of his letters ; but it was
no such thing. The president could a marched on foot
twenty miles a day then, and only let him been at the

head of my Downingville company and he 'd a whole
British regiment scamper like a flock of sheep.

But you see the trouble ont was, there was some difficulty between I and Mr. Van Buren.   Some how or
other Mr. Van Buren always looked kind of jealous at
me all the time after he met us at New York ; and I
could n't help minding every time the folks hollered
' hoorah for Major Downing' he would turn as red as a
blaze of fire.   And wherever we stopped to take a bite
or to have a chat, he would always work it, if he could,
somehow or other so as to crowd in between me and
the president.   Well, ye see, I would n't mind much
about it, but would jest step round 'tother side.   And
though I say it myself, the folks would look at me, let
me be on which side I would ; and after they'd cried
hoorah for the president, they'd most always sing out
' hoorah for Major Downing.'   Mr. Van Buren kept
growing more and more fidgety till we got to Concord.
And there we had a room full of sturdy old democrats
of New Hampshire, and after they had all flocked
round the old president and shook hands with him, he
happened to introduce me to some of 'em before he did
Mr. Van Buren.   At that the fat was all in the fire.
Mr. Van Buren wheeled about and marched out of the
room looking as though he could bite a board nail off.
The president had to send for him three times before
he could get him back into the room again.   And when
he did come, he didn't speak to me for the whole evening.   However we kept it from the company pretty
much ; but when we come to go up to bed that night,
we had a real quarrel.   It was nothing but jaw, jaw,
the whole night.   Mr. Woodbury and Mr. Cass tried
to pacify us all they could, but it was all in vain, we
didn't one of us get a wink of sleep, and shouldn't if
the night had lasted a fortnight.   Mr. Van Buren said
the president had dishonoured the country by placing a
military major on half pay before the second officer of
the government.   The president begged him to consider that I was a very particular friend of his ; that I

had been a great help to him at both ends of the country; that I had kept the British out of Madawaska away down in Maine, and had marched my company clear from Downingville to Washington, on my way to South Carolina, to put down the nullifiers; and he thought I was entitled to as much respect as any man in the country.

This nettled Mr. Van Buren peskily. He said he thought it was a fine time of day if a raw jockey from an obscure village away down east, jest because he had a major's commission, was going to throw the vice president of the United States and the heads of departments into the back ground. At this my dander began to rise, and I stepped right up to him; and says I, Mr. Van Buren, you are the last man that ought to call me a jockey. And if you 'll go to Downingville and stand up before my company with Sargeant Joel at their head, and call Downingville an obscure village, I'll let you use my head for a foot-ball as long as you live afterwards. For if they wouldn't blow you into ten thousand atoms, I'll never guess again. We got so high at last that the old president hopt off the bed like a boy; for he had laid down to rest him, bein it was near daylight, though he couldn't get to sleep. And says he, Mr. Donaldson, set down and write Mr. Anderson at Portland, and my friend Joshua Downing at Downingville, that I can't come. I'm going to start for Washington this morning. What, says Mr. Cass, and not go to Portsmouth and Exeter and round there! I tell you, says the president, I'm going to start for Washington this morning, and in three days I'll be there. What, says Mr. Woodbury, and not go to Portland, where they have spent so much money to get ready for us! I tell you, says the president, my foot is down: I go not a step further, but turn about this morning for Washington. What, says I, and not go to Downingville, what will Uncle Joshua say? At this the president looked a little hurt; and says he, Major Downing, I can't help it. As for going any further with such a din as this about my ears, I cannot, and will not, and I am resolved not to budge another inch. And sure enough the president was as good as his word, and we were all packed up by sunrise, and in three days we were in Washington.

And here we've been ever since, battling the watch about the next presidency. Mr. Van Buren says the president promised it to him, and now he charges me and the president with a plot to work myself into it and leave him out. It's true I've been nominated in a good many papers, in the National Intelligencer, and in the Munch Chunk Courier printed away off among the coal diggers in Pennsylvany, and a good many more. And them are Pennsylvany chaps are real pealers for electing folks when they take hold ; and that's what makes Mr. Van Buren so uneasy. The president tells him as he has promised to help him, he shall do what he can for him ; but if the folks *will* vote for me he can't help it. Mr. Van Buren wanted I should come out in the National Intelligencer and resign, and so be put up for vice president under him. But I told him no ; bein it had gone so fur I wouldn't do nothing about it. I hadn't asked for the office, and if the folks had a mind to give it to me I wouldn't refuse it. So after we had battled it about a fortnight, Mr. Van Buren found it was no use to try to dicker with me, and he's cleared out and gone to New York to see what he can do there.

I never thought of getting in to be president so soon, though I 've had a kind of bankering for it this two years. But now, seeing it's turned out as it has, I'm determined to make a bold push, and if I *can* get in by the free votes of the people, I mean to. The president says he'd rather I should have it than any body else, and if he had n't promised Mr. Van Buren before hand, he would use his influence for me.

I remember when I was a boy about a dozen years old, there was an old woman come to our house to tell fortunes. And after she 'd told the rest of 'em, father says he, here's Jack. you have n't told his fortunes yet.

and I dont spose it 's worth a telling, for he 's a real
mutton-headed boy. At that the old woman catched
hold of my hair, and pulled my head back and looked
into my face, and I never shall forget how she looked
right through me, as long as I live. At last, says she,
and she gin me a shove that sent me almost through the
side of the house, Jack will beat the whole of you. He
'll be a famous climber in his day, and wherever he sets
out to climb, you may depend upon it, he will go to the
top of the ladder. Now, putting all these things together, and the nominations in the papers, and the 'hoo-
rahs for Major Downing,' I dont know what it means.
unless it means that I must be president. So, as I said
afore, I'm determined to make a bold push. I 've writ
to Col. Crocket to see if I can get the support of the
western states, and his reply is, ' go ahead.' I shall
depend upon you and uncle Joshua to carry the state
of Maine for me ; and, in order to secure the other
states, I spose it will be necessary to publish my life
and writings. President Jackson had his life published before he was elected, and when Mr. Clay was a
candidate he had hisn published. I 've talked with the
president about it, and he says, publish it by all means,
and set the printer of the Portland Courier right about
it.

So I want you to go to work as soon as you get this,
and pick up my letters, and begin to print 'em in a
book ; and I 'll set down and write a history of my
life to put into it, and send it along as fast as I can get
it done. But I want you to be very careful not to get
any of them are confounded counterfeit letters, that
the rascally fellers have been sending to the printers,
mixed in long with mine. It would be as bad as breaking a rotten egg in long with the good ones ; it would
spile the whole puddin. You can tell all my letters,
for they were all sent to you first.

The president says I must have a picter of me made
and put into the book.—He says he had one put into
his, and Mr. Clay had one put into his. So I believe I

shall write to Mr. Thatcher that prints the little journal paper in Boston, and get him to go to some of the best picter-makers there, and get them to do me up some as slick as they can. These things, you know, will all help get the free votes of the people ; and that 's all I want. For I tell you now, right up and down, I never will take any office that does n't come by the free votes of the people. I 'm a ginuin democratic republican, and always was, and so was my father before me, and uncle Joshua besides.

There's a few more things that I want to speak to you about in this letter but I'm afraid it will get to be too lengthy. That are story that they got in the newspapers about my being married in Philadelphy is all a hoax. I aint married yet, nor I shant be till a little blue-eyed gal, that used to run about with me, and go to school and slide down hill in Downingville is the wife of President Downing. And that are other story that the President give me a Curnel's commission jest before we started down east, is n't exactly true. The President did offer me one, but I thanked him, and told him if he would excuse me, I should rather not take it, for I had always noticed that Majors were more apt to rise in the world than Curnels.

I wish you would take a little pains to send up to Downingville and get uncle Joshua to call a public meeting, and have me nominated there. I'm so well known there, it would have a great effect in other places. And I want to have it particularly understood, and so stated in their resolutions, that I am the ginuin democratic republican candidate. I know you will put your shoulder to the wheel in this business and do all you can for me, for you was always a good friend to me, and, jest between you and me, when I get in to be President you may depend upon it you shall have as good an office as you want.

But I see it's time for me to end this letter. The President is quite comfortable, and sends his respects to you and uncle Joshua. I remain your sincere friend,

MAJOR JACK DOWNING.

LETTER LVII.

*Cousin Ephraim's account of converting "dimocrats"
into federals, and making them change sides.*

Downingville, State of Maine, August 12, 1833.

To Cousin Major Jack Downing, at Washington city, or else
gone long with the President down to the Rip Raps. To
be sent privately in the Portland Courier.

DEAR COUSIN JACK.—I 've got something pretty
heavy on my mind that I want to tell ye about, and ask
your advice, and may be I shall want you to lend me a
hand a little.   I 've been watching politics pretty snug
ever since I was a little boy, and that's near about forty
years; and I believe I know most as much about it as
uncle Joshua, although he's twenty years older than I
be. Now about this republicanism and federalism, I've
minded that it always keeps changing, and always has,
ever since I can remember.   And I've minded tu it
most always keeps going round one way; that is, the
young federalists keep turning dimocrats, and the old
dimocrats keep turning federalists.   What it's for I
dont exactly know, but that's the way it goes.   I spose
a man, on the whole, is n't hardly fit to be a dimocrat
after he gets to be fifty years old.   And here is old
uncle Joshua in the Post Office, he's got to be about
sixty, and he's hanging on to the dimocratic side yet,
like the tooth-ache; and it begins to worry me a good
deal.   I think it's high time he went over.   You know
Downingville has always been a ginuin republican
town, and I want it should always go according to the
usages [I think that's what they call it] of the dimocratic party.

When it gets to be time for an old dimocrat to go over
on the federal side, I believe the Argus always puts 'em
over.   You remember there was old Mr. Insley in Portland, and old Gineral Wingate in Bath, as much as a

N

dozen years ago, were some as big republicans as there was any where about. Well, they got to be considerable old, and had been in office sometime, so the Argus took and clapt 'em right over on to the federal side. And you know there was Mr. Holmes, he was a whapping great republican. But he begun to grow old, and so the Argus put him over. And there was Mr. Sprague; he was such a nice dimocrat every one said it was a pitty to put him over. But bein he 'd been to Congress sometime, the Argus would n't hear a word, but shoved him right over.

And this summer the Argus is putting of 'em over considerable younger on to the federal side. It has put Judge Preble over, and Judge Ware, and Mr. Mitchell the Post Master at Portland, and he is n't near so old as uncle Joshua, and it has put Mr. Megquier over, only think, such a young man as Mr. Megquier, that's only been in the Sinnet three or four years. Now dont you think, according to dimocratic usage, it is high time old uncle Joshua was put over. I wish you would jest write to the Argus and have it done, for I feel a good deal worried about it.

And as soon as it comes out in the Argus that he is fairly over, I want you to tell the President that uncle Joshua is a federalist, and have him removed from the Post Office, for it would be an everlasting shame to have the Post Office in Downingville kept by a federalist.

N.B. If uncle Joshua should be removed I wish you would use your influence to get the President to give the office to me; for next to Uncle Joshua I spose I've done more for the republican party than any man in Downingville. I can have a recommendation from Sargent Joel and all the company. By attending to this you will much oblige your friend and cousin,

EPHRAIM DOWNING.

LETTER LVIII.

The President commences a conversation about ME *and*
DANIEL.

Washington City, Sept. 14, 1833.

To the Editor of the Portland Courier, away down East, in
the State of Maine.

MY DEAR OLD FRIEND,—Its got to be a pretty considerable long while now since I've writ to you, for I never
like to write, you know, without I have something to
say.—But I've got something on my mind now, that
keeps me all the time a thinking so much that I cant
hold in any longer. So jest between you and me I'll
tell you what 'tis. But I must begin a little ways be-
forehand, so you can see both sides of it, and I'll tell
you what 'tis as soon as I get along to it.

You see I and the President has been down to the
Rip Raps a few weeks to try to recruit up a little; for
that pesky tower away down East like to did the job for
the old Gineral. So, after we got things pretty much to
rights here, we jest stepped aboard the steamboat and
and went down to the Rip Raps. That are Rip Raps is
a capital place; it is worth all the money we ever paid
for it, if it was for nothing else only jest to recruit up
the Government. It is one of the most coolest places
in the summer time that you ever see. Let a feller be
all worn out and wilted down as limpsy as a rag, so that
the doctors would think he was jest ready to fly off the
handie, and let him go down to the Rip Raps and stay
there a fortnight, and he'd come up again as smart as a
steeltrap. The President got recruited up so nicely,
while we were down to the Rip Raps, that ever since
we got back till two or three days ago, he has been as
good natured and sociable as ever I should wish to see
a body. And now I'm coming, pretty soon, to what I
was going to tell you about, that bears so heavy on my
mind.

You see the President likes every morning after the breakfast is out of the way, to set down and read over the newspapers. and see what is going on in the country, and who's elected and so on So when we've done breakfast, we take the letters and papers that come from the Post-Office, and go away by ourselves into the great East Room where we can say jest what we've a mind to, and nobody not hear us, and the President sets down in his great arm rocking-chair and smokes his segar. and I set down by the table and read to him. Last Monday morning, as I was reading over the papers one arter another, I come to a Pennsylvania paper and opened it, and, says I, hullow, gineral, here's a speech of Mr. Webster at Pittsourg, as large as life. Ah, said he; well, let us hear what Daniel has been talking to them are Pennsylvany and Ohio chaps about. So I hitched back in my chair, and read on. And by and by I begun to get into the marrow of the story, where he told all about Nullification, and what a dark time we had of it last winter, and how the black clouds begun to rise and spread over the country, and the thunders of civil war begun to roll and rumble away off to the South, and by and by how the tempest was jest ready to burst over our heads and split the country all into shivers, and how, in the very nick of time, the President's Proclamation came out and spread over the whole country like a rain-bow, and how every body then took courage and said the danger was all over. While I had been reading this, the President had started up on his feet, and walked back and forth across the room pretty quick, puffing away and making the smoke roll out of his mouth like a house a fire; and by the time I had got through, he had thrown his segar out of the window, and come and sot down, leaning his elbow on the table and looking right in my face. I laid the paper down, and there he sot looking right at me as much as five minutes, aud never said a word; but he seemed to keep a thinking as fast as a horse could run. At last, said he, Major Downing, were you ever told that you resembled Daniel Webster ?

Why, Gineral, says I, how do you mean, in looks or what?

Why perhaps a little of both says he, but mostly in looks.

Bless my stars, says I, Gineral, you dont mean to say that I am quite so *dark* as he is.

Perhaps not, says he; but you have that sharp knowing look, as though you could see right through a millstone. I know, says he, that Mr. Webster is rather a dark looking man, but there is n't another man in this country that can throw so much *light* on a dark subject as he can.

Why yes, says I, he has a remarkable faculty for that; he can see through most any thing, and he can make other folks see through it too. I guess, says I, if he'd been born in old Virginny he'd stood next to most any body.

A *leetle* afore 'em, says the Gineral, in my own way of thinking. I'll tell you what 't is Major, I begin to think your New Englanders aint the worst sort of fellows in the world after all.

Ah well says I, seeing is believing, and you've been down that way now and can judge for yourself. But if you had only gone as fur as Downingville I guess you would have thought still better of 'em than you do now. Other folks may talk larger and bluster more, says I, but whenever you are in trouble, and want the real support in time of need, go to New England for it and you never need to be afraid but what it will come.

I believe you are right, says the Gineral; for notwithstanding all I could do with my proclamation against nullification, I believe I should have rubbed hard if there had been no such men in the country as Major Downing and Daniel Webster.

But this nullification business is n't killed yet. The tops are beat down, but the roots are alive as ever, and spreading under ground wider and wider, and one of these days when they begin to sprout up again there 'll be a tougher scrabble to keep 'em down than there has

N 2

been yet; and I 've been thinking, says he, and he laid
his hand on my shoulder and looked very anxious, I've
been thinking says he, *if you and Daniel*——and here
the door opened and in cometh Amos Kendle with a
long letter from Mr Van Buren about the Bank and the
safety fund and the Government deposites and I dont
know what all; and the President's brow was clouded
in a minute; for he always feels kind of pettish when
they plague him about the safety fund. I have n't had
any chance to talk with him since, there 's so many of
'em round him; and I 'm as uneasy as a fish out of
water, I feel so anxious to know what the President was
going to say about me and Daniel. I shall watch the
first chance when I think it will do to talk with him,
and find out what he was going to say. I cant hardly
sleep a nights, I think so much about it. When I find
out I'll write to you again.

Send my love to the folks up in Downingville when
you have a chance.

I remain your sincere friend,
MAJOR JACK DOWNING.

———

LETTER LIX.

The conversation about ME *and* DANIEL *concluded.*

Washington City, Sept. 30, 1833.

To the Editor of the Portland Courier, away down east in the
State of Maine.

MY DEAR FRIEND,—Havn't you been in a terrible
kind of a pucker ever since my last letter to you, to
know what the President was going to say about me
and Daniel? If you havn't, I have. I never felt so uneasy for a fortnight hardly in my life. If I went to bed

I couldn't sleep, and I've got up and walked the floor as much as half the night almost every night since.— I've wished the Bank to Guinea more than fifty times, for there's been such a hubbub here about the Bank this fortnight past, that I couldn't get a moment's chance to talk with the President about any thing else. We'd have cabinet meetings once in awhile to see about moving the deposites, and Mr. Duane and Mr. Cass and Mr. McLane would talk up to the President so about it, that he'd conclude to let 'em alone and do nothing about it, and let Congress manage it jest as they'd amind to. And then we'd go home and Mr. Kendle would come in and talk the matter over, and read some great long letters from Mr. Van Buren, and get the President so confused that he would lose all patience a most.

But Mr. Kendle is the master feller to hang on that ever I see; he's equal to the tooth ache. And he talked and palavered with the President till he finally brought him over, and then the President put his foot down, and said the deposites should be moved whether or no. And then the botheration was to see who should move 'em. The President told Mr. Duane to do it; but he said his conscience wouldn't let him. Then the President told Mr. Taney to take Mr. Duane's place, and see if his conscience would let him. Mr. Taney tried it and found his conscience went easy enough, so Mr. Duane packed up and went home to Philadelphy. We were all dreadful sorry to loose Mr. Duane, for he was a nice man as you will see one in a thousand. It's a pity he had such a stiff conscience; he might have staid here in the Treasury jest as well as not, it it hadn't been for that.

But this storm about the Bank begins to blow over, and the President's got in a manner cooled down again. This morning after breakfast we took the papers and letters jest as we used to, and went away into the east room to read the news and chat awhile; and it really did my heart good to see the President set down once more looking so good natured in his great arm chair smoking his segar. After I had read over the news to him awhile, and got him in pretty good humour, I made bold to out with it, and says I Gineral, there's one question I want to ask you.—And says he, you know Major, I always allow you to ask me any thing you're a mind to, what is it? Well says I, when we had that talk here about a fortnight ago, you begun to say something about me and Daniel; and jest as you got into the middle of it, Mr. Kendle came in and broke it right off short as a pipe stem. It's been running in my head ever since, and I've been half crazy to know what it was you was going to say. Well, let us see, says the Gineral, where was it I left off; for this everlasting fuss about the Bank has kept my head so full I can't seem to remember much about it.

Why says I, you was talking about nullification; how the tops were beat down a little, but the roots were all running about under ground as live as ever, and it would n't be long before they'd be sprouting up again all over the country, and there'd be a tougher scrabble to keep 'em down than ever there had been yet; and then you said *if I and Daniel*—— and there that plaguy Kendle came in, I've no patience with him now when I think of it, and broke it right off. Ah, now I remember, says the Gineral, now 'twas. Well, says he, Major Downing, it is a solemn fact, this country is to see a blacker storm of nullification before many years comes about than ever it has seen yet; the clouds are beginning to gather now; I've seen 'em rolling over South Carolina, and hanging about Georgia, and edging along into old Virginny, and I see the storm's a gathering; it must come, and if there is n't somebody at the helm that knows how to steer pretty well, the old ship must go down. I aint afraid, says he, but what I can keep her up while I have the command, but I'm getting to be old and must give up soon, and then what'll become of her I dont know. But what I was going to say was this; I've been thinking if you and Daniel, after I give up, would put your heads together and take charge of her till the storm has blown over, you might save her. And I dont know who else can.

But how do you mean, Gineral, says I? Why to speak plain, says he, if nullification shows its head, Daniel must talk and you must fight. There's nothing else will do the job for it that I know of. Daniel must go into the Presidential chair, and you must take command of the army, and then things will go straight. At this I was a little struck up; and I looked him right in the eye, and, says I, Gineral, do you mean that Daniel Webster ought to be President after you give up? Certainly, says he, if you want to keep the country out of the jaws of nullification. But, says I, Gineral, Daniel is a federalist, a Hartford Convention federalist, and I should like to know which is worst, the jaws of nullification, or the jaws of federalism. The jaws of a fiddle-stick! said the President, starting up and throwing his segar out of the window as much as two rods; but how do you know, Major Downing, that Daniel is a federalist? Because, says I, I've heard him called so down east more than a hundred times. And that's jest all you know about it, says he. Now I tell you how 'tis, Major Downing, Daniel is as thorough a republican as you be, or as I be, and has been ever since my Proclamation came out against nullification. As soon as that Proclamation came out Daniel came right over on to the republican ground and took it upon his shoulder and carried it through thick and thin where no other man in the country could have carried it. Says I, Gineral, is that a fact? And says he yes, you may depend upon it, 'tis every word truth. Well says I, that alters the case a little, and I'll write to Uncle Joshua and the editor of the Portland Courier and see what they think of it, and if they think it's best to have Daniel for President we'll have him in, and I'll take my turn afterwards: for seeing the people are bent upon having me for President I wont decline, though if it is thought best that I should wait a little while, I wont be particular about that.

I'm willing to do that which will be best for the country.

So I remain your loving friend,

MAJOR JACK DOWNING.

LETTER LX.

Being the genuine letter of old Mr. Zophar Downing,
' amost eighty-three yere old.'

{ Uppington, Western Resarve
{ Tuesday, June 5, A. D. 1833, N. S.

To my NEFFU JOHN DOWNING :—I am got to be amost eighty three Yere old, and I'm in my eighty third Year now, and its so long since I have took any Pen in my hand to write any thing nor a Letter to any Boddy living for now going on a very long Time. And what makes it particular bad for me is that my Fingers is got stiff with Rhumatiz and cold, and is all Thums, as much as tho they was froze in the Winter.—Your Ant is sick abed ; she ketch'd cold some Time in Aperil, and I dont know when she will git over it ; she is in her eighty second Year most as old as I be, we are both very old and prety much done with this World, so to speake. I did not ever expect to write any more Letters to my Frinds because I'm in my eighty third Year and am too old most to write Letters. But you writ a Letter to me from the Citty of Washington and it was throw'd out of the Stage Wensday as it drove by. And when I redd about your goin to take the President of these United States to Downingvile then I said to your Ant my dear I must try and write an Answer to Jonny's Letter.

I was jeest about as old as you be John when the Great Washington died, 14 day of December, and was with him and spoke with him seventeen year before, when he left the Army and wisht I might live many yeares, and what you writ to me makes me think a good deal of that time. I shant forget it to my dyin day— but I hope you wont have Ardint Sperrits in your Town on the occasion. I dont drink any more Flip nor Tody sence 17 August A. D. 1831 and am better fort, and hope Brother Joshua has stopped. Two of my Cows was lost last year by Destemper and one of Mr. Doolittles who lives opposite, is a hard worken Man. Some Destemper was here this yere but I follerd what was said in the Temperance Almanick and they was cured in time to git over it. I desire that my Brother Joshua woud write a Letter to me to let me know whether he is going to make out as well with his Turnips as he did 3 year ago, he wrote to your Ant about it. I tryde that Plan here, but it dont do in this Soil, it is to dry most of it. Your Aut tells me she dont think Brother Joshua can be so strong of his Age as I be, seeing he hant writ any ot us since that Account of his Garding Sauce turnin out so remarkable good that year.

It is thirty-two years ago next month since I was in Downingville, how is Deacon Wiloby and his family and his daughter Sooky was uncommon humersome, but your ant always used to say she thot Sooky was a little too fond of seeing people perlite and that she was to espirin for Downingvile when she was young and a comely child. I thank you John for some newspapers you sent to me last when so much was writ about the President and the Vice President, one spell I was afeared that the poor salvages in Georgia State was agoin to suffer till the great Proclamation to the Nuliphiers as they are called which you sent to me, but I hope they are not now, they are a sufferin Peeple certin. If you do take the President east I hope there is no boddy but what will treat him with respect. You know John I dont know much about politix, but I know something of my bible, and I hope I shall alwais read in it while I continue to live, and it says in the 2nd Book of Samuel, about Absalom's setting by the gate and shakin hands and kissin every boddy that passed by, and whisperin in their ears what he would do if he was king, and you know mor about the Vice President, and I ask you if that man aint adoin so too, and if it is not some boddys duty to speak to the President about it. But my hand shakes somes writin so much, and give my love and ants to all our relations and to the neighbours of yours that I used to know. I am your loving Uncle,

ZOPHAR DOWNING.

LETTER LXI.

BANK REPORT.

To the Editor of the New York Daily Advertiser.

Major Downing's Official Report on the United States Bank Published by 'authority.'

Rip Raps, August 4th 1833.

DEAR SIR,—I have jest got here after examinin the Bank ; and it was the toughest job, ever I had in my life. The Gineral was so bent on my doing it, that I had to 'go ahead,' or I'd sneak'd out the first day. I was nigh upon a week about it, figerin and siferin all the while. Mr. Biddle see quick enuf it was no fool's journey I come on ; and I made some of his folks scratch their heads, I tell you. I gin 'em no notice of my comin, and I jump'd right in the thickest on 'em there one day, when they were tumblin in and shellin out the munny like corn. 'Now,' says I, 'my boys, I advise all on ye to brush up your multiplication tables, for I am down upon you with alligation, and the rule of three, and vulgar fractions ; and if I find a penny out of place, the Gineral shall know it. I'm no green horn, nor member of Congress, nor Judge Clayton, nor Mr. Cambreleng, neither,' says I. As soon as Mr. Biddle read the letter the Gineral sent by me, says he, ' Major, I m glad the Gineral has sent some one at last that knows something, and can give a strait account,' and with that he called all the Bank folks, and tell'd 'em to bring their books together. ' Now,' says he, ' Major, which eend shall we begin at first.' ' It makes no odds which,' says I, ' all I care about is to see if both eends meet; and if they don't, Mr. Biddle,' says I, ' it's all over with you and the Bank—you'll all go, hook and line,' —and then we off coats and went at it. I found some of them are fellers there plagy sharp at siferin. They'd do a sum by a kinder short Dilworth quick as a flash. I always use a slate—it comes kinder natural to me ; and I chalk'd her off there the first day and figur'd out nigh upon 100 pretty considerable tuf sums. There was more than three cart load of books about us, and every one on 'em bigger than the Deacon's family Bible. And sich an etarnal batch of figerin I never see, and there wasn't a blot or scratch in the whole on 'em

I put a good many questions to Mr. Biddle, for the Gineral gin me a long string on 'em ; and I thought some would stagger him, but he answered them all jest as glib as our boys in Downingville do the catakize, from the chief ' eend of man,' clean through the petitions—and he did it all in a mighty civil way too, ther was only one he kinder tried to git round, and that was—how he came to have so few of the Gineral's folks among the Directors until very lately? ' Why,' says he, Major, and Major,' says he (and then he got up and took a pinch of snuff and offered me one) says he, ' Major, the Bank knows no party ; and in the first go off, you know, the Gineral's friends were all above matters of so little importance as Banks and Banking. If we had but a branch in Downingville,' says he. ' the Gineral would not have had occasion to ask such a question,' and with that he made me a bow; and I went home and took dinner with him. It is plagy curious to hear him talk about millions and thousands;

O

and I got as glib too at it as he is; and how on earth I shall get back agin to ninepences and four-peace-hap-penies, I can't tell.

Arter I had been figerin away there nigh upon a week, and used up four or five slate pencils, and spit my mouth as dry as a cob, rubbin out the sums as fast as I did them, I writ to the Gineral and tell'd him it was no use ; I could find no mistake; but so long as the Bank was at work, it was pretty much like counting a flock of sheep in a fall day when they are jest let into a new stubble, for it was all the while crossing and mixing, and the only way was, to lock up all the Banks, and as fast as you can count e'm black their noses.

'Now,' says I one day to Squire Biddle, 'I'll jest a leok at your moneys bags, for they tell the Gineral you han' got stuff enuf in the Bank to make him a pair of spectacles; none of your rags,' says I, 'but the real grit;' and with that he call'd two or three chaps in Quaker coats, and they opened a large place about as big as the 'east room' and sich a sight I never see—boxes, bags and kags, all full, and should say nigh up-on a hundred cord.   Says I, 'Squire Biddle, what on earth is all this for? for I am stumped.'   'O,' says he, 'Major,' that's our Safety Fund.'   'How you talk!' says I.   'Now, says I, 'is that all genwine?'   'Every dollar of it,' says he.   'Will you count it, Major?' says he.   'Not to day,' says I; 'but as the Gineral wants me to be particular, I'll jest hussle some 'em;' and at it I went, hammer and file. It raly did mo good, for I did not think there was so much real chink in all creation.   So when I got tired, I set down on a pile, and took out my wallet, and begun to count over some of the 'safety fund' notes I got shaved with on the grand tower.   'Here,' says I, 'Squire Biddle, I have a small trifle I should like to barter with you; it's all "safety fund,"' says I; 'and Mr. Van Buren's head is on most all of 'em.'   But as soon as he put his eye on 'em, he shook his head.   I see he had his eye teeth cut. 'Well,' says I, 'it's no matter;' but it lifted my dander considerable.

'Now,' says I, Mr. Biddle, I've got one more question to put to you and then I'm through. You say your bills are better than the hard dollars; this puzzles me, and the Gineral too. Now, how is this?' 'Well,' says he, 'Major, I'll tell you : Suppose you had a bushel of potatoes at Downingville, and you wanted to send them to Washington, how much would it cost to get them there?' 'Well, says I, 'about two shillins lawful—for I sent a barrel there to the Gineral, last fall, and that cost me a dollar freight.' 'Well,' say, 'suppose I've got potatoes in Washington jest as good as yours, and I take your potatoes in Downingville, and give you an order to receive a bushel of potatoes in Washington, wouldn't you save two shillins lawful by that? We sometimes charge,' says he, ' a trifle for drafts, when the places are distant, but never as much as it would cost to carry the dollars,' and with that we looked into the accounts agin, and there it was. Says I, ' Squire Biddle, I see it now as clear as a whistle.'

When I got back to Washington, I found the Gineral off to the ' Rip Raps,' and so I arter him. One feller there tell'd me I could'nt go to the Rip Raps—that the Gineral was there to keep off business ; but as soon as I told him who I was, he ordered a boat and I paddled off.

The Gineral and I have talked over all the Bank business ; he says it is not the best to publish my report, as he wants it for the message ; and it would only set them *Stock fish* nibblin agin in Wall Street. I made him stare when I tell'd him about the dollars I saw there ; and once and awhile he would rinkle his face up like a ball of ravilins ; and when I tell'd him Biddle would n't give me any of his ' Safety Fund' for any of Mr. Van Buren's that I had with me, the Gineral took out his wallet, and slung it more than five rods into the brakers.

We are now purtty busy, fittin and jointin the beams and rafters of the message ; and if Mr. Van Bu-

ren dont get back before we begin to shingle it, I guess
that his Safety Fund will stand but a poor chance.

The Gineral don't care much about having his head
for a sign board, but says he, ' Major, when they put
my head on one eend of a Bank Bill, and Mr. Van Buren's on tother eend, and "promise to pay Andrew
Jackson," and then blow up, it's too bad—I won't allow it—it shant be.' The Gineral says, if he allows
Amos Kendle to make his report about the State Banks,
it is but fair to let me publish mine about Square Biddle's Bank. So I am getting mine ready.

We have a fine cool time here, and ain't bothered
with Office seekers ; we can see 'em in droves all along
shore, waitin for a chance. One fellow swam off last
night to get appointed to some office—the Gineral thinks
of making him minister to the King of the Sandwich
Islands, on account of their being all good swimmers
there.   Yours,

           J DOWNING. Major, Downingville
                    Militia, 2d Brigade.

_____

LETTER LXII.

Giving some account of Peleg Bissel's Churn.

Rip Raps, Aug, 17, 1833.

To the Editor of the New York Daily Advertiser.

MY GOOD FRIEND.—"*The Government*" will leave
here on Saturday, so you must tell all our friends to
stop sending any more letters here. We go strate to
Washington, to put things to rights there for winter.

I and the Gineral have got things now pretty considerable snug ; and it is raly curious to see how much more
easy and simple all the publick affairs go on than they

did a spell ago, when Mr. Adams was President. If it warnt for Congress meetin we cou'd jest go about pretty much where we pleased, and keep things strate too; and I begin to think now with the Gineral, that ater all, there is no great shakes in managin the affairs of the nation. We have pretty much all on us been joggin about now since last grass; and things are jest as strate and clear now as they was then. The Gineral has nigh upon made up his mind, that there is no use to have any more Congress. They only bothers—they wou'd do more good to stay at home, and write letters to us tellin what is goin on among 'em at home. It would save a considerable sum of money too; and I 'm also sartin that there is a plagy raft of fellows on wages that dont earn nothin. Howsoever, we are goin on makin things more simple every day, and we once and a while nock off a pretty considerable number of cogg wheels and trunnel heads.

The Gineral says he likes things simple as a mouse trap. But what I like most is, he wont have no one about him who outranks me, so there is me and Major Barry, and Major Smith, and Major Earl, and Major Donaldson, and Major Lewis, and Major Eaton;—and the major part of a purty considerable of a man to do the rinting and tell the folks where we be, and once and a while where the land sales and contracts be too. There is a enuff on us to do all that's wanted. Every day jest after breakfast, the Gineral lights his pipe, and begins to think purty hard, and I and Major Donaldson begin to open letters for him ; and there is more than three bushels every day, and all the while coming We dont git through more than a bushel a day; and never trouble long ones, unless they come from Mr. Van Buren, or Mr. Kindle, or some other of our great folks. Then we sort 'em out, jest as Zekel Bigelow does the mackerel at his Packin Yard, for tho' there are plagy many more sorts than he finds among fish, we only make three sorts, and keep three big baskets, one marked 'not red,' another 'red, and worth nothin,' and another

O 2

'red and to be answered.' And then all the Gineral
has to do is to say, 'Major, I reckon we best say so and
so to that,' and I say 'jest so,' or not, as the notion
takes me—and then we go at it.

We keep all the Secretaries, and the Vice President,
and some District Attorneys, and a good many more of
our folks, and Amos Kindle, moving about; and they
tell us jest how the cat jumps. And as I said afore, if
it warnt for Congress meetin once a year, we'd put the
Government in a one horse wagon and go jest where we
liked.

The Gineral was amazingly tickled t'other day. Peleg Bissel—(you know Peleg, who is all the while whitlin, and sawin, and makin clocks, and apple parers, and
churns, and lives nigh Seth Sprague's School house,
down to Downingville,) well Peleg sent the Gineral a
new churn of his own invention; and he calls it the
'Jackson Churn,' he wants a patent for it. The cute
critur says, in his letter to the Gineral, that that are
churn is jest like his government—its only got one
wheel, and a smasher; and that it will make more butter than any other churn, and out of eny most any thing.
The Gineral is so well pleased with it, he will set and
turn it nearly all day. Says he, 'Major, I like this ere
churn amazingly, that Bissel is a knowin fellow. If
that churn had been made by Congress, it would have
more than fifty wheels and springs, and make no more
butter ater all. Major,' says he, 'tell Peleg I thank
him; and send him a patent.'

And so I did; and I telled him in the letter, that the
Gineral would keep his churn in the hall of the white
house, to let folks see that it did n't require as many
cogwheels to make butter as they think on, and then
when they come up chamber, in the Cabinet Room, and
find ony me and the President, they'll understand it
the better. When the Gineral come to sign this letter,
'well,' says he, 'Major, that's just what I was thinkin
on. We get every day an everlastin bach of letters
from Mr. Van Buren and Amos Kindle, and they are

so plagy jagged, that we cant make 'em fit exactly with some others, eny most as jagged, from the South and West, and all from our folks too. One wants one thing, and one wants t'other. Some of our folks down South say, if the Bank is put down, we shall all be split up into splinters there. And jest so, ony t'other way, they say, we shant find in a week any of our folks north if the Bank is rechartered, and some talk of the Nullifiers in Georgia going for Mr. Van Buren, and that we must look out sharp, and not do nothin agin 'em. And some say that are tower of Mr. Webster away West, and his speeches, bother some on 'em plagily. I was a little stumped for a spell myself; and I tell'd the Gineral, says I, 'Gineral, if you expect me to satisfy all these folks, you're mistaken, we cant do it,' says I.— 'Well then,' says he, 'we must send for Mr. Van Buren.' This kinder nettled me, and says I, 'Gineral, you ha'nt forgot that are churnal ready'—'no, no,' says he, 'we'll stick to that Major.' 'Well then,' says I 'do you think that Mr. Van Buren will use that are churn?' he keeps his bread buttered,' says I, 'by more wheels than that are churn's got.' 'Well Major,' says the Gineral, 'he is a plagy curious critter, ater all—he'll make wheels turn sometimes right agin one another, yet he gits along—and when he lets his slice fall, or some one nocks it out of his hand, it always somehow falls butter side up'—'well,' says I, 'Gineral, dont you know why?' 'not exactly,' says he, 'Major'—'well,' says I,—'I'll tell you—he butters both sides at once,' says I. The Gineral drew his face all into a rumple for about a minute, and then he snorted right out.

The Gineral talks of goin to the Hermitage next spring—he says he thinks he has done enuf for the country—and I think so too—he says I may go along with him or stay and lend Mr. Van Buren a hand— we'll say something about this in the Message.

Yours as before,

J. DOWNING, Major.
Downingville Militia, 2d Brigade.

LETTER LXIII.

The Public Crib at Washington.

Washington, August 30, 1833.

To Mr. Dwight—New York Daily Advertiser.

MY GOOD OLD FRIEND,—Ever since we got 'the Government' back here from the Rip Raps, we have been as busy as if we was all on us cocking hay jist afore a shower.

I tell'd you some time ago that I and the gineral was fittin and jointin the beams and rafters of the message, but almost every day some plaguy new motion comes in from Mr. Van Buren, and some other of our folks, and we have to chizzle new mortises, and run new braces and string pieces, so that I begin to think it will look curious enuf when its done. The gineral says he dont care how it fronts, only he is determined to show a sharp corner to the nullifiers. We shall have a good deal to say about the *Grand Tower;* there is nothin since the 8th of January at New Orleans tickles the gineral half so much. Every time we talk about it, the gineral gits right up, and says he, 'Major, I only wish I was fifty years younger, and then,' says he, 'give me the yankees east of Horse Neck, and I'd like no better sport than to have nullification all over the rest of creation.'

When things dont go right, and the gineral gits a little wrathy, if I only tell him the yankees are ready to back him, he is as firm as granite. It would make you crawl all over to read that letter we writ to France, when we come to hear that the king there kinder suffled round that bill we drawed on him. 'He wont pay it, wont he ?' Says he—'Major, what do you think of that ?'—'why,' says I, 'Gineral, I think its a nasty mean action—and a rascally one too,' says I. 'Well,' says he, 'that's enuff,'—and then we writ the letter,—its jest like Zekel Bigelow's speech—it cuts, shaves, and makes the hair fly—and if it dont bring the money, I'm mistaken.

If Mr. Livingston had stayd one week longer in York, the gineral was for sendin me right out.

The most curious part of ' the government' here, is to manage the office seekers. You see, things aint now as they was afore Mr. Van Buren's time, then it was kinder divided around among the departments.

The post-master gineral appointed all the post-masters and their folks. The secretary of the treasury appointed all the folks in the custom-houses, and all folks who collected money. These two had an everlastin batch of fellers to appint, and made them feel pretty considerable big, and then the war secretary had a good slice in appointing the cadets, and Ingen agents, and all the contracts was kinder sifted round among the departments ; and so by the time a new president was to be made, some of these secretaries was a leetle bigger than the president himself. Now this is the way they kinder jockied Mr. Adams, who got to be the smallest man at Washington, by lettin other folks plant his corn, and do his huskin ; and afore he knowd it, his own field was all in weeds—and theirs well howed, rich and clean as a whistle.

But things aint so now, w've got ony one crib, and that's a whapping one too, and ony one door to it ; and when we shell out our corn, we take good care and know well who gets it, and where he is going to plant it ; and that aint all—we make 'em agree about the *Huskin Frolic*,* for that's the best ont arter all.

The longer I am in ' the government' the more I larn. But I must allow that of all the inventions I've hearn on of Mr. Van Buren's, this is about the slickest.

There is ony one thing wantin, and that he is tryin for pretty hard—and that is the bank. If he can ony get that in the crib too, Virginy fences would n't stop our cattle.

Ony think what an everlastin raft of fellows we

---

* The major, we presume, means the elections, or Hustings, by this metaphor.

should have—all the presidents and cashiers, and clerks, and money counters, about the crib, from Downingville to New Orleans !—and that aint the best ont; we would have a branch alongside every post-office to keep our postages safe.

I should like this well enuf I was sartin I and the gineral and Mr. Van Buren was to be here all the while, to keep a good look out on the crib door. But the gineral talks of going hum to put the Hermitage to rights; and I am in the notion that congress is a leetle too strong for 'the government' when the gineral aint in it—and I shall go with him. I am eny most fag'd out myself, and I begin to think with the gineral, I have done enuf for the country.

We are lookin for Amos Kindle now every hour. He writ the gineral tother day, and teld him my 'Bank Report' warn't true, and that I must have got a loan of Squire Biddle. Now that's jist the way with some folks. What they dont know they guess at; and it's jest so with old Miss Crane, who keeps the tavern this side Downingville—jist as sure as any one goes by without stopping, the old critur says, 'There goes so and so, and has got no money, too, and he knows I would n't trust him.'

Howsumever, no one can make the gineral rathy with me. He knows I am the best friend about him; whenever they gets things in any kind of a twist or a snarl, says he, 'Major, do you unravel that, I 'm the big wheel and you are the smasher,' says he; and then we jist give Peleg Bissel's churn a turn or two and all is right.

You don't print my letters right—you git some words wrong and spell 'em bad. Jist so the printers sarved the gineral's letters too; and folks thought he didn't know nothin, till we got to Cambridge, where they made a doctor on him.

Your friend,

J. DOWNING, Major,
Downingville Militia, 2d Brigade.

LETTER LXIV.

Preparation of the Message.

Washington, 2d Nov. 1833.

To my old friend, Mr. Dwight, of the New York Daily Advertiser.

The Congressmen are jest beginnin to arrive here, and I suppose in a short time we shall have them here as thick as huckleberries; and the Gineral is brushin round now, and says the Message must be finished and painted off hand, and we are all as busy as bees in gittin it dove tailed together; and after next week, the Gineral says, there cant be any more alterations. It is the first message I ever had any hand in; and tho' I say it, I guess you will say it is about as complete a thing as ever was sent express any where.

I have been to work on it ever since we was at the Rip-Raps; and tho' it has been sometimes all pulled to bits, to git in some notions we did n't think on, yet it will look pritty slick, I tell you when it 's done; and we will lay on paint enuf to kiver up all the cracks and seams.

We shall give a pritty good lick at the Bank, and won't leave as much on 't standing as would make a good sized oven. It is curius now to see how easy it is to build up, or nock all to bits, any thing on paper. Now jest see about the Bank. There it stands in Chestnut street, with its hundred cord of specie, and its cart load of books; and its branches here and there, and all busy and full of clarks, and directors, and folks in Europe. and all about creation dealin with it; and the brokers in Wall street all busy about it; and Biddle's bills goin about, and most folks thinkin they are better than hard dollars; and all the old men and women holdin the stock, supposin it will go up agin as high as they paid for it; and I and the Gineral, and Amos Kindle,

and Mr. Van Buren, talkin over it; and one line in the
Message nocks it all into kindlin wood. For you see
wnen 'The Government' says a thing must be jest so!
there is no help for it. We can't stand to chat about
trifles. The Gineral has smashed three pipes the last
time we talked aoout it. 'Biddle and the Bank must be
smashed,' says he, ' Major;'—and so smash they go,
Congress or no Congress.

The next thing was the Ingins. Here the Gineral is
at home, and I don't pretend to say nothin for I never
did like an Ingin, and never can. The Cherokees
give us a good deal of trouble in Georgia last year; but
the Gineral took sides with Georgia, because he had a
good many friends there, and Mr. Van Buren had too;
for that State was the ony one that nominated him Vice
President a spell ago; and if he had got in there, and
Mr. Crawford President, who was ailin all over with
some plaguy *appleplexy*—I and the Gineral would never
have been hearen on arterwards. But no matter.—The
Gineral says he didn't make that treaty with the Cherokees; and it was made so long ago, he has enymost forgot it: and treaties oughtent to last forever.   But this
treaty with the Creeks in Alabama he did make, and he
knows all about it; and he means to stand by it, and
turn all the squatters off the land in Alabama, jest as
they wanted him to do in Georgia; but he would n't.
There is trouble enuf about it, I tell you; and you aont
know nothing about it in York. But the Gineral is
tickled to death about it; and as soon as he saw the
Proclamation of the Governor of Alabama, you never
see a critur so spruced up as the Gineral was. Major,
says he, we shall have another Nullification this Congress, arter all. You need 't say much about it, says
he, in the Message,—we'll keep that for a Proclamation.
Well, says I, Gineral, you are a master hand at gettin
into trouble. But, says he, Major, aint I a master one
in gittin out of one, says he?

We've got an old trunk up chamber full of troubles—
old Laws, and Treaties, and Contracts, and State

Claims; and whenever we want any powder, all we 've got to do is to open that, and look among old papers and get up a row in no time. The Gineral likes this a leetle better that I do; for the most of the labor falls on me, and the ony way I can git rid of it, is to make our folks down stairs do it, if I see it gives any of 'em a boost with his party—for I dont care nothin about any thing here but the Gineral; and if I can git him threw this Congress, its pretty much all I care about, and he too; for arter that I'm goin with him to the Hermitage, for I expect by that time there wont be much more left of us than our beards and shoe strings.

Your friend,

J. DOWNING, Major.

Downingville Militia, 2d Brigade.

LETTER LXV.

The Major's account of the Hubbub at Washington about the Bank.—Some further particulars about the Major and Daniel.—And sundry matters respecting Nullification, and South Carolina.

From the Portland Courier of Saturday.

Washington City, Sept. 30, 1831.

To the editor of the Portland Courier away down east in the state of Maine.

MY DEAR FRIEND,—Have you n't been in a terrible kind of a pucker ever since my last letter to you, to know what the President was going to say about me and Daniel? If you have n't, I have. I never felt so

P

uneasy for a fortnight hardly in my life. If I went to bed I could n't sleep, and I've got up and walked the floor as much as half the night almost every night since. I've wished the Bank to Guinea more than fifty times, for there's been such a hubbub here about the Bank this fortnight past, that I could n't get a moment's chance to talk with the President about any thing else. We'd have cabinet meetings once in awhile to see about moving the deposites, and Mr. Duane and Mr. Cass and Mr. M'Lean would talk up to the President so about it, that he'd conclude to let 'em alone and doo nothing about it, and let Congress manage it jest as they'd amind to. And then we'd go home and Mr. Kendle would come in and talk the matter over, and read some great long letters from Mr. Van Buren, and get the President so confused that he would lose all patience a most.

But Mr. Kendle is the master feller to hang on that ever I see; he's equal to the tooth ache. And he talked and palaver'd with the President till he finally brought him over, and then the President put his foot down and said the deposites should be moved whether or no. And then the botheration was to see who should move 'em. The President told Mr. Duane to do it; but he said his conscience would n't him.—Then the President told Mr. Taney to take Mr. Duane's place, and see if his conscience would let 'em. Mr. Taney tried it and found his conscience went easy enough, so Mr. Duane packed up and went home to Philadelphia. We were all dreadful sorry to lose Mr. Duane, for he was a nice man as you would see one in a thousand. It's pity he had such a stiff conscience; he might have staid here in the Treasury just as well as not if it had n't been for that.

But this storm about the Bank begins to blow over, and the President's got in a manner cooled down again. This morning after breakfast we took the papers and letters jest as we used to, and went away into the east room to read the news and chat awhile; and it really did my heart good to see the President set down once more looking so good natured in his great arm chair, smoking his segar. After I had read over the news to him awhile, and got him in pretty good humor, I made bold to out with it, and says I, Gineral, there's one question that I want to ask you. And says he, you know, Major, I always allow you to ask me any thing you're a mind to, what is it? Well, says I, when we had that talk here about a fortnight ago, you began to say something about me and Daniel; and jest as you got into the middle of it, Mr. Kendle came in and broke it right off short as a pipe stem. It's been running in my head ever since, and I've been half crazy to know what it was you was going to say. Well, let us see, says the Gineral, where was it I left off; for this everlasting fuss about the Bank has kept my head so full I can't seem to remember much about it.

Why says I, was you talking about nullification; how the tops were beat down a little, but the roots were all running about under ground as live as ever, and it wouldn't be long before they'd be sprouting up again all over the country, and there'd be a tougher scrabble to keep 'em down than ever there had been yet; and then you said *if I and Daniel* —— and there that plaguy Kendle came in, I've no patience with him now when I think of it, and broke it right off. Ah, now I remember, says the Gineral, how 'twas. Well, says he, Major Downing, it is a solemn fact, this country is to see a blacker storm of nullification before many years comes about, than ever it has yet; the clouds are beginning to gather now; I've seen 'em rolling over South Carolina, and hanging about Georgia, and edging along into old Virginny, and I see the storm's a gathering; it must come, and if there isn't somebody at the helm that knows how to steer pretty well, the old ship must go down. I aint afraid, says he, but what I can keep her up while I have the command, but I'm getting to be old and must give up soon, and then what'll become of her, I don't know.—But what

I was going to say was this; I've been thinking if you
and Daniel, after I give up, would put your heads together and take charge of her till the storm has blown
over, you might save her.   And I dont know who else
can.

But how do you mean, Gineral, says I ?   Why to
speak plain, says he, if nullification shows its head, Daniel must talk and you must fight.   There's nothing else
will do the job for it that I know of.   Daniel must go
into the Presidential chair, and you must take command
of the army, and then things will go straight.   At this
I was a little struck up and I looked him right in the
eye, and says I, Gineral, do you mean that Daniel Webster ought to be President after you give up ?   Certainly, says he, if you want to keep the country out of
the jaws of nullification.   But, says I Gineral, Daniel
is a federalist, a Hartford Convention federalist, and I
should like to know which is worst, the jaws of nullification, or the jaws of federalism.—The jaws of a fiddle-
stick ! says he ; but how do you know, Major Downing,
that Daniel is a federalist ?   Because, says I. I've heard
him called so down east more than a hundred times,
over and over.   And that's jest all you know about it,
says he.   Now I tell you how 'tis, Major Downing,
Daniel is as thorough a republican as you be, or as I be,
and has been ever since my Proclamation came out
against the nullification.

As soon as that Proclamation came out Daniel came
right over on to the republican ground and took it upon
his shoulder and carried it through thick and thin where
no other man in the country would have carried it.
Says I, Gineral, is that a fact?   And says he yes, you
may depend upon it, 'tis every word truth.   Well says
I, that alters the case a little, and I'll write to Uncle
Joshua and the editor of the Portland Courier and see
what they think of it, and if they think it's best to have
Daniel for President we'll have him in, and I'll take
my turn afterwards : for seeing the people are bent upon having me for President I wont decline, though if it

is thought best that I should wait a little while, I wont be particular about that. I'm willing to do that which will be best for the country.

So I remain your loving friend,

MAJOR JACK DOWNING.

LETTER LXVI.

Washington, 4th Dec. 1833.

To my old friend, Mr. Dwight, of the New York Daily Advertiser.

My last letter tell'd you that the Message I had been to work on for some time was jest finished—but the very next day we had to take it all to bits, and spring to and write enymost the hull of a new one, for we found we had gone too much into particulars, especially about the counts; and letters from Mr. Van Buren, advised us to say as little about such matters as possible, for Congress would only make us tell pretty much the hull on't over agin—and the best way was to say little at first, and trust to luck and chance afterwards. As soon as the Gineral came to know of this, says he, 'Major you must look out and keep in that latin about the Bank any how.' So we kept that in, but it was plagy troublesome to make it work well with the rest on't, for when you come to make English on't, it reads that the Gineral would have taken the Bank by the throat right off, if he thought he could make that latin pill operate afore the charters expire—and then agin he says the Bank does wrong in bringing its business to a close so rapidly as it is now doing. There is one thing however that's true enuf, for seein that Judge Marshall is a stubborn know nothin kind of critur, and would have a finger in givin the Bank that pill the Gineral speaks of it in latin, I don't believe it would have operated before the charter expired, if it had 40 years

P 2

more to run—so there is more wit and cunnin in what the Gineral says than folks think for.

There was another thing puzzled us tu a trifle about the Bank. Last year when we thought it had no rale chink in it, the Gineral thought best to take the deposites away from it, but since I tell'd the Gineral in my Bank report there was more than a hundred cords of the rale grit, we had to say in the Message they had too much

The post office accounts was the next bother; and that puzzled all on us peskily. But we got round that by very lucky discovery; and you see by the Message there has been an error in keepin the counts in the post office ever since General Washington's time, and every post master Gineral, up to Major Barry's time, never found it out; and it was so curious that he took nigh upon five years to git at it. But its all clear now, for he is an amazin shark fellow at siferin. We struck out all about the *grand tower*, for Clay has been over the same ground, and Mr. Van Buren thought it was best to say nothin about it. And it was thought best too to say nothin about the Nullifiers, for some of Mr. Van Buren's friend's in Georgia headid by Crawford are gettin up nullification there, worse than Calhoun's last winter; and it maks all the difference in the world when you come to see that ones own friends are doin what our enemies did afore.

As soon as we sent the Message to Congress, we set about gittin up a supper for all our folks who had been to work out, and we had a grand time, all our Majors was there. The Gineral was so beat out, he didn't stay long; but some on 'em kept it up all nigh day light.

We had some rale good songs tu; and one of our Majors is a plagy sharp singer. I got a copy of one on 'em; but I haint got time now to send you the hull on on't, so I'll jest give you 3 verses only.

Come comrades one and all
Here assembled in the hall
Let us sing of times past, present and to come.

We have everything at stake,
And our fortunes yet to make,
And the public good is now-a-days " a hum."

Times past have all gone by
And old laws are "all my eye"
The *present* and the *future* we are sure in
When the Gineral's time is up.
We'll fill again the cup,
And drink to Amos Kindle and Van Buren.

We have no one to thank
For a discount at the Bank,
Since we've got the public money from Nick Biddle
And as we alone have ernt it
We'll use it as we want it
Security is now all fiddle diddle.

I wish you would tell folks to stop callin me *Jack*
Downing—twas well enuf when I wasnt quite as much
up in the world as I now be, and it was jest so with
Mr. Van Buren—folks would keep callin him " *Mat;*"
but it warnt right, and it aint good manners nuther.
And there is another thing I dont like; but I dont care
so much about it (for I aint asham'd of any letter I
ever did write) and that is printin in a Book all the
Letters I *first* writ, and mixing up other Letters and
Sam Patch, and callin some of my Letters to you coun-
terfits. As soon as I get the Gineral threw this Congress, I'll turn tu and get my Letters all together that
I writ to you, beginnin with the *grand tow'r*. Major
Earl is drawn my likeness, and the Gineral's and Mr.
Van Buren's and the most of our folks for me. He is
a master hand at it; and Zekil Bigelow tells me if I'll
give him the copyright, he'll new shingle our old barn
for nothin. How comes on your book about the Hartford convention? The Gineral wants you to send him

a copy on't as soon as it is done—he wants to see how nigh Yankee Nullification comes to Nullification now-a-days.

Yours, &c.

J. DOWNING, Major,
Downingville Militia, 2d Brigade.

LETTER LXVII.

The Major's conversation with the President on the subject of the Bank, the currency, his cabinet, the proclamation, Messrs. Clay, Taney, and other matters.

Washington, Dec. 14, 1832.

To my old friend, Mr. Dwight of the New York Daily Advertiser.

We have got business enuf now on our hands, I tell you ; and nigh upon every day we have a squall that brings all hands to the helm. We have had fair wind so long, that few on us know exactly how to steer now a days, when every wind comes right in our teeth. I hain't had my coat off since congress met ; and the gineral says we must watch them fellows closely. "Keep a sharp look out, Major," says he, "on Clay— he is a *bold, independent* fellow, and will speak out his notions if the devil stands at the door ; and if he had the people with him," says the gineral, "as I have, there is no tellin what trouble he would give us; make as good a gineral as ever was. But it will never do *to trust that man with power.*" "Very well," says I, "gineral—but plague on't," says I, "the critur some how keeps law on his side all the while." "That's true enuf," says the gineral, "and therefore we must keep a sharper eye on him, and the time is come, now Ma jor, when we must all on us try our popularity—for when the law is agin us, we shan't have nothin else to stand on. There is nothin," says the gineral, "like war times, Major—for then, when those troublesome fellows talk about law, I' give 'em Martial Law, and that makes short work ont."

Just ater breakfast yesterday, I and the gineral had a high time together. I had been expectin every day to see the bank come out with a *reply ;* and I tell'd the gineral, says I, ' Gineral, I'm afraid we'll git a stumper from Philadelphy one of these days, that will nock us all into kindlin wood. But he kept sayin there was no fear of that. ' Why,' says he, • Major you forgit that we first give the bank a most mortal weltin 3 years ago and left em no other defence than to print reports, and speeches ; and that show'd they hadn't much spunk ; and we have been criplin on em ever since. And when I see they began to stagger, I give em our hull battery, and opened upon em in flank, front, and rear our sharp shooters headed by that amazin cute little district attorney open'd first on em. Then come my proclamation—and then my message—and then Mr. Tany's report—and the globe all the while throwin shells and rockets. ' Why' says the gineral—gittin up and taken his hickory, and givin it a whack on the floor—' if the bank stands all that racket, Major, its tuffer than a pepperage log. "No, no Major," says the gineral, "don't you fear that the bank will ever say a word in reply—it's as dead now." says the gineral, " as a skin'd racoon." And the words want out of his mouth, afore in come a hull bundle of letters and newspapers, and the first thing I see among 'em was the " Bank reply." " Now," says I, "gineral, here's trouble!—here's the very thing," says I, " I've been afraid of all the while.' The gineral laft a spell ; and says he, " Major, suppose you and I now jist take a bout, and you'll see how easy I can nock that reply into nothin." " Well," says I, " Gineral," its a bargain—" Now," says I, let us sit down, and you may take, says I, the globe or our dis-

trict attorney's report, or your proclamation, or your
message, or Mr. Tany's report—ary one on em,—or,
says I, come to think on't, you may take 'em all together,—for they are pretty much *all one*—and I'll take
this ' Bank reply,' and then let's see what kind of a
fight it will turn out. ' Well,' says the gineral, ' you
are a man of spunk, Major, and I like you for it : if I
make a prisoner on you, I'll treat you like a brave soldier.' ' And so will I you, Gineral,' says I, ' and if you
fall in the fight,' says I, ' Gineral, I'll bury you,' says
I, ' with the honors of war, and then we shook hands.
Now, Major, says the gineral, as I am to begin the
fight, don't you fire till I fire, '' and then we'll go threw,
shot by shot.''
    Well, says I, ''I want to know first, if I have a
right to fire back *your shot*, if they miss me, and I can
pick em up ?'' '' O, yes,'' says the gineral, '' that's fair
in war. Use the enemy's shot and shells, and guns
too, if you can, Major—*that's the true art of war*.'' The
gineral all the while kept fixing his papers all in a
string on one side the table. He put his own messages
and proclamation in the middle, and flank'd off with
our district attorney and Mr. Tany's reports ; and then
he sifted the Globe about, and called them *scouts* and
foragers—'' There,'' says he, '' Major, I am now nearly ready ; and he took off his specks, and gin em a
good rubbin, and put em on again. '' Now, Major,''
says he, '' take your station.'' And I went round tother
side, and sat down. '' Are you ready,'' says the gineral ? '' All ready,'' says I—and at it we went. The
gineral, he open'd his fire first, as agreed, and he fir'd
away from his first message—And then his 2d—then
he took the Globe, and then the reports,—and he blaz'd
away like all wrath, for an hour ; and as soon as he
stop'd to take breath. ''Now,'' says I, '' its my time,''
—and I read the reply a spell, and answered all he said
in three minits. And I gin him a look ! The gineral
twisted his face most shockin, and scratched his head
too. But he went at it agin as spunky as ever ; for he

is an amazin tuff critur in a fight, and hangs on like a snappin turtle when he gits hold.   He banged away a spell agin like all natur ; and jest as he took his specs off to give em a rub, I gin him the reply agin.   The gineral gin his face another plagy hard rumple ; and I sat waitin for him to fire agin. Says he, " Major, that's a sharp piece you are firin with there." " It's a peeler," says I, " Gineral, I tell you—but you haint got the best on't yet—it's gettin warm," says I.

" Major," says the gineral, " suppose we change batteries—let me take that reply, and you take all these documents. I like to fight," says the gineral, " when there is ten to one agin me."   " So do I," says I, " Gineral, and so we'd better fight it out as we sit."

The gineral looked a spell at his paper again ; and says he, " Major, I reckon we had better have a truce." "Not now," says I. " I've got my hand in now, and want to see the fight out."   " Well," says the gineral, " you see Major what comes when any one attempts to drive the executive ;" and with that he got up, and took off his specs, and put em in his pocket, and put on his hat, and took his hickory, and fetched a whack on the table,—" VETO," says he, "that's enuff," says I, " Gineral."

' And now,' says the Gineral, let's go and take a walk—and so we went. The Gineral didn't say nothin for more than a mile, and I nother. ' So, to rights,' says he, 'Major, every body says Money is very scarce.' ' That's true enuf,' says I, 'and it's not got as scarce as it will be afore winter is over,'—and then I tell'd the Gineral the cause on't. 'Well,' says the Gineral, 'I believe you are right; and if the worst comes to the worst,' says he, 'we'll have a new bank, and that will make money plenty agin, wont it?'—'Yes,' says I, 'I suppose so; but we can't git a new bank, Gineral, fore this ones time is out, and that's nigh three years yet; and long afore that time,' says I, 'there will be trouble enuf, as this one must all the while be collectin in its own money; and folks will fail, and be bankrupt; and then twenty new banks will do no good.' 'I don't see that,' says the Gineral. 'If we could make a new bank now,' says I, 'right off, and let it take up the business of the old one, it wouldn't make much odds. But the law wont allow that, you know, Gineral.' And just then the Gineral got in a way he has of twitchin with his suspender buttons behind; and to rights he broke one off.—'There,' says he, 'Major, here is this confounded button off again.' 'Well,' says I, that's a small matter —here is a tailor's shop,—let's go in and make him put it on—and so in we went. The tailor happened to be one of our party, and was tickled to death to see the President, and thought he was goin to git an office right off, and was plagily cut down when he come to find it was ony a button off; and so he jumped back on his board, and sat down on his heels agin, and said if the Gineral would take off his pantaloons he'd put it on in a few minutes.

I looked at the Gineral, and he looked at me—and we both looked at the tailor. 'Why,' says the Gineral, 'this is the worst thing, Major, I ever met—I'm stump'd completely! It will never do to risk walking home with this button off; for if 'tother one comes off, it's all over with me; and I sit here without my pantaloons till that fellow puts on a button, I'll kitch my death of cold! look here Major, says the Gineral, that other button is takin all the strain, and it will come off in less than five minutes—what is to be done? It seems to me Major, said the Gineral, 'that no man is placed so often in such real trouble as I am'—'yes,' says I, 'Gineral, but its fortunate for you, you always have me with you.' 'I know it, Major,' says he, 'and I hope you will be as true a friend now as ever you have been—and with that says I to the tailor, 'can't you fix things now, so as to get over all this trouble?' 'There is only one way,' says the tailor, 'and that I've stated, and another thing,' says he, 'the Gineral wants a new pair.' 'You rascal,' says the Gineral, 'you can't make a better pair, and one that fits me better, if you try a month—these panta-

loons, said the Gineral, are, better than a new pair; and
if they only had new buttons here they would last me
to my dying day.—It takes me weeks and months to
git a pair to sit easy.   I wont have a new pair,' says
the Gineral, 'that I'm determin'd on.'   'I see,' says
the Gineral, 'what you are after—you want a new
job.'

'Well,' says I, 'Gineral, let me try—and with that
I wax'd a thread, and got a new button; and whilst the
Gineral stood up, I sot down behind him, and stitched
on the button in 3 minits—the Gineral all the while
shakin his hickory at the tailor, and tellin him that he
had no more brains in his head than he had in his thim-
ble.   'You are a pretty fellow to belong to my party,'
says he; 'I should have been soon in a pritty condition,
if I had taken your advice,' says the Gineral.'   Let
me ever ketch you at the White House agin.'   So to
rights, the tailor got mad too, and said he did'nt belong
to the Gineral's party—he was a Tany-Kindle-Van-
Buren-Jackson-man; he knew which side his bread was
butter'd, and I looked plagy knowin too—it was jest as
much as I could do to keep the Gineral from smashin
him—so says I, 'come, Gineral, let's be movin; and
we went home—the Gineral all the while talkin about
his escape from an awful state, that tailor was about
getting him in.

'Well,' says I, 'Gineral, little things sometimes give
us a kink, and a notion of bigger ones; and now,' says
I, 'do you know, Gineral, we are in a scrape now pretty
much like that one we jest got out on.'   'How so?' says
the Gineral.   'Why,' says I, 'the Bank—there it is,'
says I, 'jest like your pantaloons, *better than new*;—
and only wants a new button; and some of these tailors
about us here want us to set shiverin and shakin, and
runnin the risk of gettin a rheumatiz that will last us
our lives, jest for them to get the job of makin a new
one.'

'And now,' says I, 'I guess you and I had better
disappoint 'em, as we did the tailor jest now, stitch on

Q

a new button, and things will all go smooth agin.'—
The Gineral did'nt say a word; but he got thinkin
plagey hard, till we got home agin, and he got his pipe,
and I got mine, and just as we were lighten em, says
he, 'Major, there are some fellows about us here that
pester me most desperately—we must all go as a 'Unit,'
or I must blow 'em all up and get a new set. 'W'ell
think of it,' said the Gineral, and with that, we cock'd
our feet on the mantle tree, and in less than five minits
you could'nt see no more on us than our toes.

Your Friend,

J. DOWNING, Major.

Downingville Militia, 2d Brigade.

LETTER LXVIII.

*The Major and the President again holds an important
conversation on the affairs of the nation and how
things should be conducted. The President calls the
cabinet together, and the Major prepares a paper to
to read to it which he afterwards has printed for the
good of the nation.*

To my old friend Mr. Dwight of the New York Daily Advertiser.

You know I've ben tellin you long about my fears of
many troubles—well it's bad enuf—and is goin to be
worse yet or I know nothin.   And the Gineral is beginnin to think so too.   All our folks about us here dont
feel it for they have all got fat offices—but I know the
people feel it who haint got fat offices—and until they
will speak up, things will go worse and worse—every
letter I get is full of trouble and distress—and I tell'd
the Gineral tother day, says I, Gineral we must look
into this matter now I tell you—why says he Major the

government aint to blame—every man about me says it aint his fault. Well, says I, some one did it I'm certain—things went smooth enuf, says I, till we got dablin and medlin in money matters and the Bank, and now its all heads and points, and when we say it aint our fault, says I, its pretty much like a man puttin a pole over a fence on a swivel—and after pullin one end round with a jerk, if he knocks over a dozen folks with the other end says it aint his fault—now its pretty much jist so with the Bank, says I, and if you can't see it, all I can say is, I can.

Well Major, says the Gineral, something must be done any how, for I begin to think that politics and money matters dont always work together. I'll call all our folks together, says the Gineral, and we'll have a full cabinet and look into this matter, and do you Major prepare yourself, for I'm goin to turn over a new leaf, that I'm determined on—and with that he issued orders for every man to be at the Cabinet Chamber the next day just after breakfast—and I went to work puttin down all my notions in writin, for I expected a rough time and a pretty sharp set of fellows to beat off, and thinks I as it is the fashion now-a-days to read papers to the Cabinet, I'll give 'em one that will be worth readin, and I guess it will be the last one that the Senate will ask an official copy of in one while. It took nigh upon all night to write it out—and I sprung to it, for I think the time is come to let some folks see they haint got a green horn to outwit when they try me.

And so the Gineral had 'em all up in the Cabinet Chamber yesterday, and such an overhawlin I never see—I sat all the while with one foot on the table, whitlin a piece of shingle—and the Gineral was walkin round among 'em, tellin about the troubles in money all about the country, and asking how we are to get out of the scrape—I kept an eye on most all on 'em, and both ears on pretty much the hull on 'em, and such a winzin and tangle I never see since the day all Downingville cum over to the Jackson side, and that was jist arter his

election—They thought I was determin'd the first go
off to say nothin—And to rights I heard one chap jist
behind me tell the Gineral " there was *one Major* in the
Cabinet who made pretty much all the trouble, and that
he was writin letters that went all the while agin the
rest on 'em—and if it warn't for *him* they could make
the people believe, just what they wanted—that it was
his fault that the Cabinet was obliged to shift their
ground about the Bank and cross tracks every day. If
it had 'nt been for him the deposites would have been
removed *because* there warn't no ' Safety Fund' in the
Bank, and the People been contented—and if it warn'
for *him* the government could make the people believe
that Biddle was the sole cause of their bein no money
now-a-days," and so on.   I jest stop'd whitlin a minit
and cast my eye over my left sholder, and the fellow
dodg'd behind the Gineral in a flash, and when I look'd
round the ring I found pretty much the hull on em lookin at me and there warn't a word said.

And to rights the Gineral he walk'd up to me and
stop'd right in front and look'd me strait in the face.
says he, Major you've hearn all that is said—and I
should like to know what you have to say in reply—
no man shall leave this room says the Gineral till this
trouble is cleared up—' Major' says the Gineral (and his
lip began to quiver I tell you) Major, says he, it would
take a good many men to convince me that you aint
what I have always found you—*an honest man and
a true patriot*—some folks about us have bin whisperin in my ear for a long while that you aint what
I think you are—but Major says the Gineral—I am a
soldier and so are you—and we are now all face to face
—no more whisperin says the Gineral, and he gave his
hickory a whack on the floor and look'd round the hull
ring—The country is in a trouble says he, and the
time is come for every honest man to speak out—if
there is error let it be corrected—if there is trick we
must expose it—and now Major says the Gineral, do
you set still—and if any man has any thing to say agin

you let him speak out. When they are all done—you can answer them—and with that the Gineral pull'd his own chair up to the other side of the table and laid his hickory and hat down before him, and all our folks began to nock noses in little groups here and there, and one 'em, no matter who, was as busy as a lap dog on a tranin day, smelling round from one to another to find the right man to speak first—but none on 'em seem'd to like it.—The Gineral all the while sat blinkin and lookin round at 'em all, and rumplin his face once and a while most plagily.

So to rights, this one of 'em come forward and bow'd, and says he, *Gineral,* that " our sufferings is intolerable," there is little doubt; and the question is not *how* we got *into* our present condition, but how we can best *git out of it.* I believe, says he, (turnin with a bow to every body—for he is an amazin polite cratur,) *that* is the true and only point now for discussing. " Not exactly, says I, but no matter." " Well, says he, as regards the Major, far be it from me to make any charge against him; he is decidedly the favorite of the people, and should be the favorite of every man in office who wishes to keep his office; but I would say, that I wish the Major had a higher office. I wish he was an auditor of accounts—or a receiver of public money—or a minister abroad—or an Ingin agent, or any other office in the government; but as he is now—there is no getting hold of either end of him; we can't elevate him, which I sincerely desire—we can't put him down, which no man desires. There are things in all governments—and in this in particular, that requires cookin up before the should be served with it; but the Major hands the dishes over to the people raw and uncook'd, and lets every man dress his own dinner—this is not right.

And then, again, he is an enemy to party, and thinks that politicians shouldn't meddle in money matters, when we all know that none of us would now be here without office, and that *office* aint worth a fig without *money;* and so it comes to this—we've got a party, and a good strong one; and that party must keep all the offices, and the control of all the money; for, without money, the offices wont be good for nothin—and, without offices the party will be all scattered: look at my own state, see how things work there; and just so they would hero. We must have the Bank—we can't do anything without it. It is all good enough enough if we could get Biddle and his friends out of it—but seein we have tried that and can't succeed, this must go down, and then we'll have a new one after our own fashin—unfortunately, some will suffer—because this one must, I suppose, collect its debts and wind up—but what is the sufferings of a few in trade, compar'd to the breaking up of a *political party,* now all hitched together, think of us all going back again to practice law—and you, Mr. Auditor, to keeping a school—and you, Mr. Secretary, to keeping a shop—and you to ploughing—and you to plantin corn, and you to digging potatoes—and you to printin newspapers.—" And you, Major," says he, " what would become of you?"

I began to crawl all over, and was just goin to say something, but I thought I wouldn't tell he got through; and he reeled it off for more than an hour pretty much in the same way about things in general, and Major Downing in particular—and as soon as he stopt, I got up and says I, has any body got nothin more to say? No one said a word. Says I, is all that is said put in writin?—for then there will be no mistake; no turnin corners; no dodgin afterwards. " O no," says he, " there is no necessity to put any thing in writin of this nature—that ain't my way," says he. " I have always said I don't like to get into the newspapers." " Well," says I, "that's just where we differ—what I'am goin to say now, say I, is all in my pocket in black and white—and with the Gineral's permission, says I, I'll read it to the members of the Cabinet, and then I'll git it printed, and then all on you can read it, and every man shall have a copy on't except Clay and the rest of the Senate—for tho' the law says they are a part of the government, they ain't got no business with any paper read to the Cabinet—ain't that law, says I, Gineral?" The Gineral nodded his head, and that was enuf; and says he, "Major, do you read that paper; I know you well enuf to know it will be an honest view of things, and I don't care whose toes you tread on. I have no interest in these matters further than to do my duty— if any fellows have misled me, I advise 'em to keep an eye on my hickory."

And then I took out my papers from my pocket and went at it; and I didn't mince matters I tell you. The Gineral sat restin his elbows on the table with his chin in both hands and lookin straight in my face the hull time, ony once in a while he'd take his hickory and whack it on the table when any one muttered and whispered; and as soon as I got to the end on't, then come a buz and a maxin; and the Gineral got up and fetched another whack on the table with his hickory, enuf to loosen ones eye teeth.

Now, says the Gineral, I've hearn both sides, and the people will shortly hear it too. If they say the Major is right, I wont oppose them any longer; if they say the Major is wrong, then we'll go on as we now go; and now, says he, Major, git that paper printed, and the only favor I ask of you is not to sent an official copy out to the Senate if they ask one;—and with that, I and the Gineral bowed off the Cabinet, and the Majors, and the rest of the government; and we turned to readin letters from all quarters, all full of money troubles and distress, enuf to give one the cholera morbus; for as I said afore one is just about as bad as t'other.

I'll send you to-morrow or next day, the paper I read to the Cabinet, and the rest of the government, for you to print It's too long for this letter, and you can ask Zekel Bigelow, if he haint stop'd payment, to pay for the expense of printen on't, and tell him for me if his head is above water, its more than can be said of most folks—and he better hold on to all he's got, and ride

out the storm if he can. His last letters to me say
things are shockin bad in Wall street, but the worst
there aint as bad as things are away West and South,
and they will be worse yet, if the people don't decide
pretty soon, as the Gineral says, whether I am right or
wrong.—For its the people's business now, and the
Gineral is waiten for 'em.

Your Friend,

J. DOWNING, Major,

Downingville Militia, 2d Brigade.

LETTER LXIX.

MAJOR DOWNING'S OFFICIAL COMMUNI-
CATION TO THE CABINET.

*Read to the Cabinet, and majors, auditors, and under-
secretaries, and sub-postmasters, and the rest of the
Government, on 26th day of December, A. D.* 1833
*—and printed for the use of all the citizens from
Downingville to New Orleans, along the sea coast,
and up the Missippi and Missouri, and so down the
Lakes, and across by the Erie Canal to Albany, and
along by the midde rout over New Jersey, Pensylvany,
and Maryland, to Washington—and away agin to
all parts of creation, and to every body.*

GINERAL—and Gentlemen of the Cabinet, and the
rest on you here present, composin the Government—
I speak to you as a man standin right between you and
the people—what I am goin to say aint calculated to
make any on you change your opinion, so much as to
make you know mine—you have pretty much all on you

had your turn, and now comes my turn—if any thing I say has sharp corners and scrapes the skin a leetle, it is because I haint had time to file the edges smooth. I'll give you my notions pretty much as you ged bread from the Bakers, and leave you to slice it or chunk it as best suits you; and every man can butter his own slice just to please his fancy—that aint my business so much as it is hisn.

We are met here not only to fix on some plan to get the country out of trouble, but to see how it got into trouble; and I am goin to say a little on both pints. When a chimbley smokes at the rong eend with the wind at the north east, some folks may content themselves with openin windows and doors, to let the smoke out, but my notion is that the safest plan is to see into the cause on't, and correct it—so that the chimbley will only smoke at the right eend, let the wind blow any way.

Now there is a few things we must look into a little, and then we will know more about em, and I am goin to examine—

What kind of a critur the bank of the United States raly is.

Whether its nature is to do good or evil to the country, and then wind up with

Matters and things in general.

Twenty years ago the country was in trouble, and fill'd up with all kinds of bank paper—nigh upon as bad as old Continental—and a good deal was a little worse. If any body aint old enuf to remember that time, and wants to see what kind of money I mean, let him go to the Treasury, and Mr. Taney can show him nigh a million and a half of dollars, not worth the cost of the paper and ink used every year in makin a report on't—but this is ony a drop compar'd to what would be now there of the same kind of stuff if it had'nt been for the Bank of the United States. All our wise folks of that day said we must have a Bank of the United States, and a good big one. One strong enuf to do the work well, and to clear out all this trash—and so this Bank was made, and the first thing was, as there was a very little rale money in the country, the Bank, went and bo't a good jag on't in Europe, and went to work here clearin away jest as we do our fields in the Spring.

It was a pretty dirty job to do so I tell you, and the Bank did'nt get through with it without scratchin and smuttin its fingers pretty considerable; and that warn't the worst on't for the Bank. The Government made the Bank agree to pay fifteen hundred thousand dollars for the privilege of doing this work, and made it agree to take care of the people's money in all parts of the country, and to pay it here and there wherever the Government told 'em to pay all the pensions, and to do every thing in the money way without chargin any thing for it to the Government. This was a pretty tuff bargain for the Bank—for all it got in return was to have the keepin of the money, and when the Government did'nt want it the Bank might lend it out. It took a good many years afore the Bank got things to work smooth. It was like a whappin big waggon that wanted a good many horses to drag it, and as it had a valuable freight in it, it wanted none but the best kind of horses—real Conestogas—and it warnt every one who knew how to drive such a team. The owners of this waggon found that out—for some of the first that they got came plagy nigh oversetting it. So to rights they got Squire Biddle. I suppose they thought that seein that the folks in Pennsylvany have the best and strongest horses and the biggest waggons, they ought to know best how to guide 'em. Well, they made a pretty good guess that time—for ever since they told the Squire to take the lines, they haint lost a linchpin or broke a strap; and there warnt no complaints made agin him by the folks on the road, or the country.

All the other waggoners liked the Squire amazingly, he was always ready to give 'em a lift when he found them in the mud, and whenever they got short of pro-

vender, the Squire never refused to turn out some of
his to keep their horses from suffering. Every thing
was goin on better and better, and every body said at
home and abroad there warnt such a team in all creation. Well, about four years ago we began to pick a
quarrel with the Squire, and its been goin on every year
pretty much after this fashion. The first go off some
of our folks wanted the Squire to change some of his
leadin horses—they said the breed warnt right—he
ought to put on the lead some Albany trotters—that
they were the best horses on the lead he could have.
The Squire did'nt like to change----he said the horses
he had, knew the road as well as he did, and they
would'nt bolt nor kick up, and when they came to up
hill work he could depend on 'em.

Then again our folks wanted the Squire to change
harness—they said they had new patent collars, and a
horse could pull as much agin with 'em as with the
old fashion'd collars. Well the Squire didn't like that
notion nother. So to the rights they told the Squire
he must give up the lines—well that he wouldn't do he
said, without orders from the owners of the teams—
they had appointed him, and so long as they kept him
there, he would go along and do his duty, jest he had
done—and it warnt right to keep stoppin him everyday
on the road, and trying to make him try new plans.

And with that, all our folks made a regular battle on
the squire—some took away out of his waggon a part of
the bags and boxes, and divided it round among the
drivers of others waggons, who was mixin in the scuf-
fle too, and away they crack'd off with it. Some
undertook to cut the squire's traces, they thought they
was only leather and rope traces; but the squire was
too deep for 'em, for his traces was all chains kivered
with leather, and so they spilt their jack-nives. Some
went on a-head and rolled stones in the road, and dug
deep holes, and tried all they could to make the square
upset, and threw stones and mud at him and his horses,
but the squire kept on his horses didn't flinch, and as

they had drag'd the big waggon over worse roads in the
day, they went along without accident. Well now it
turns out that all the waggons that drove off so with a
part of the squire's load are in trouble, for the first
piece of muddy road, they all stuck fast, and there they
are now. One wants the other to give him a pull and a
lift; but they say they all want lifting—the squire has
just come up with 'em, and now they want him to hitch
on to 'em and drag 'em all out together; but he says
that's impossible, the most he can do is to take back the
load they took from his waggon, and then perhaps they
can git out of the mud; but it is more than his team
can do, and he wont run the risk of breakin his harness
or injure his horses to drag 'em all out together. Well
now that's just about the condition of things, and the
longer they remain so, the worse it will be—the longer
horses and waggons stand knee and hub deep in mud,
the less able they'll be to git out on't.

And I'll leave 'em there a spell, and we'll take a look
into the natur of the Bank, and what it really is, for
to hear some folks about it, one would think it was a
most shocking monster, and that it was pretty much
nothin else but squire Biddle, when it is no more the
squire than that big waggon is, not a grain more. Look
at this long list of names ; well these are the owners of
the Bank—here we see in the first place the nation owns
one-fifth, and the rest is scattered round, as you see
here, among an everlastin batch of folks all about this
country, and some in forin countries; and I am glad
to see on the list here old widows and old men, and
trustees of children, who haint got no parents livin and
all our own people, they put their mony in the stock
of this Bank for his safe keeping—not to speculate—
and just so with the innocent foreigners, and the best
on't is they have paid our folks a pretty high premium
for every dollar on't—well these are folks then that
compose the Bank.

Now what do they want this Bank managed?—the
business of the Bank is to loan money, and is jest for

all the world like any rich man whose business is to loan out his money; is it his interest to dabble in politics or to let politicians dabble with him? not an atom on't. I never knew one of your rale politicians who ever could pay his debts, and they aint the kind of folks, people like to deal with any who may have got money to loan; they know that talking politics, and gettin things into snarls jest to answer party purposes aint the way to pay interest nor principal nother, and politicians in a Bank are the worst folks in the world for the owners of the Bank, for the most on 'em haint got mony of their own to lend, but they are plagy ready to loan other folks' money to brother politicians of the same party.

No no, a man who has got his mony loan'd out (and its jest so with a Bank) want to see every body busy and industrious and mind their business and increase their property, for then they will be able to pay interest and principal too: they dont like to see things all mixed up with politics and people quarrellin and disputin, and when they do, they git the money back in their pockets agin as soon as they can, for they know that politics aint profitable business.

Then it comes to this, that if the Bank is what I have said it is (and its nothin else,) it aint such a monster as some folks try to make us think it is, instead of being a dangerous monster. I see and I know every body else must see, who dont squint at it, but looks it strait in the face; that its natur is jest like the natur of any man who has got property in the country, and that is to have every thing go on in harmony and with industry and honesty and accordin to law; no jangles and tangles and talkin politics in porter houses and bar rooms, hurrain for this man, and pulling down that man; that kind of work dont clear up new lands nor plough up old ones, it dont keep the hammer goin, and the wheels turnin; and dont pay interest nor principal nother.

R

But some on you say the bank has too much power,
and that Squire Biddle might do a good deal of mischief if he would. Well, there is my old friend. Capt.
Elihu S. Bunker, of the steam-boat President, runnin
betwixt New York and Providence—he's got about sich
another monster—there is no tellin what a " dangerous
monopoly" of power that crittur got in that are boat.
I was lookin into it when I came on with him a spell
ago, and he was showin me how he managed it.   If he
was to fasten down the kivers of them two mortal big
copper kettles he has got in his boat, and blow his bel-
lesses a spell, he would smash every thing for more
than 50 acres round—Does any body want to know
why he don't do it—he has been in a steam-boat as
long now as the bank's been goin and haint scalded no
body—but he can do it in a minit if he chuses—well I'll
tell you why he don't—*it aint his interest* and he don't
own no more of the boat than Squire Biddle does of the
bank—the owners of the boat employ him to manage it
because they know he understands his business.   He
knows if he didn't watch over their interest they'd turn
him out—and jist so the owners of the bank would sarve
Squire Biddle.   And that aint all, Captain Bunker
knows if he hurts any body with his boat he'd run a
chance of hurtin himself too—he knows too that it is the
interest of his owners not to have any accidents aboard
any boat—for if people git scalded in one steam boat,
they'll keep clear of all on 'em—and though some folks
think banks aint like steam boats I can tell 'em that in
the main thing they are exactly alike—for unless folks
have got confidence in 'em and feel safe in 'em they aint
worth ownin—but when they all go on and meet no accidents, they are pirty good property—and the largest,
and strongest, and cleanest, and quietest, and best
managed git the most business.   Now I think that's
enuf about dangerous monopolies for a spell.

Let us now see what the bank is about, and what we
've been about.

Deacon Goodenou—Has been in that bank as one of

its directors off and on ever since it was a bank, and I
have heard him say 50 times, (and he's a man to be de-
pended on) he never heard a word about politics in it
till about 4 years ago---and it all came from our sendin
every year since that time, some rale politicians to help
the other 20 directors to manage the bank---the first go
off, the deacon says, they thought best to keep quiet,
and make no stir about it ; for it was pretty much like
finding skunks in the cellar---the best way was to let
'em alone, if they'd keep there, and run the chance of
their goin out when they found there warn't no eggs to
suck---but when they undertook to cum up chamber
and smell about in all the cupboards, it was time to
snub 'em---and then came trouble ; and that's jist about
the way now ; and the deacon says, and he is about
right, that politicians in a bank are jist as bad as
skunks in the cellar---there aint one grain of difference.

Some on you say we dont want a bank *now*---well
that may be so---but when I got up this mornin it was
plagy chilly till I got my coat on---now I am warm and
it may be I dont need a coat---but I think if I take my
coat off I'll feel chilly agin---and I am so certing of this
I wont make a trial ont.

Some on you say the owners of this bank haint got
no right to a recharter---they have had it long enuf--i
and its time now to have a new shuffle and cut---wel
that aint my notion and I'll tell you why--tho' this
bank was chartered for twenty years---it had a good
right to believe we would renew its charter if it be
haved well and did as duty---jist as a congressman has
a right to expect his constituents will send him to congress agin if he behaves well---and its a good way to-
keep folks strait and make em do their duty---but if we
are to knock this bank down and have a new shuffle
and cut, then I say that them folks who make money
out of a rise of stock in the new bank, ought to pay the
loss that all these old folks and young children will suffer by nocking down the old bank---to say nothin about
the innocent foreigners who put their money in this

bank; thinkin it was safe. And let me tell you another thing---the longer a bank stands, and the older it gits, the better folks abroad and at home like it---people who have got money to lend don't like changes--- and particularly government changes. Would any on you like to lend folks money in South America? and do you think any of them governments could make a bank that folks would have any confidence in? I dont think they could---jist because they keep choppin and changin every year.

Will any on you say that it aint a good thing for a country to make folks all about think it is a safe one to lend mony to? aint good credit worth nothin?

Well, how does any man in trade git credit, and make folks think him safe to trust? Will he break up his stand every year, and change his business, and try new plans? I say that aint the way, and no man ever prospered after that fashion; but when he finds things go well with him, he hang on; or else he haint got no wit in him.

Now, my notion is, that none on us alone can make folks all about creation think we are safe folks to trust. But all on us together can do so; and that is the reason a good big bank can manage this for us. Folks abroad know the bank; and the bank know us; and so we can manage things through the bank better than we can alone.

Some on you say it aint right to pay interest to foreigners---that when we git money from foreigners, they keep drainin us of interest. Well, that is all chalk and water. Now I know we have got an everlastin new country to clear up yet; and if an honest industrious man can git a few hundred dollars lent to him, he can go and buy a good many acres, and clear it up, and sell it to these very foreigners, who are all the while coming out here to settle among us, and they pay fifty times more for it than the land first cost; and so our folks go on borrowin, and can well afford to pay interest, and find themselves in a few years with money to lend too. And as long as this business goes on, I for one am willing to say to foreigners, as the Cape Cod fisherman says to the fish, when he gets on the hook. and is pullin him in---"So long as you hold on one eend, I will t'other." But folks abroad who have money to lend, don't know our folks who go on new land: and a good many on old land nother. But they know our bank, and our canals, and rail-roads, and we sell 'em the stock, and make 'em pay good premiums too : and our folks can lend their money to our farmers.

But if we go on, and nock down this bank when its charter is out, and bring trouble on the country, foreigners say, "Aha! there's trouble there!"---back they come with their stock, and git their mony, and keep it; and all our prosperity is nock'd in the head! We charter'd this bank for 20 years; and so we do canal companies, and rail-road companies; but did we mean when the time was up, to nock 'em all up too, and say we don't want no bank, nor a canal, nor a rail-road? It aint common honesty to say so; and I won't shuffle and cut with you after that fashion; for make what I might by a new shuffle, I would be asham'd to look one of these innocent foreigners in the face---to say nothin of this long list of widows, and orfans, and trustees of estates, and old folks, many on em, when they bought the stock at a high premium, I suppose never thought about the charter, or how long it had to run but trusted to the government. And now if you can chizzle them out of their property, as you will by puttin down this bank, jest to git a new shuffle and cut at a new one---without turnin as red as a beet when you meet em, I for one say I can't, and I won't.

And now I'm most done---if I have trod on any one's toes, it aint so much my fault as hisen; for I tread the the strait line, and tread ony on toes that stick out beyond the line, and that's too often the case with folks now-a-days in offices.

I've telled you now pretty much my notions; and

1 tell you for the last time you have made a mistake, and that's no disgrace to any man unless he tries to stick to it after he knows he has made it. If you don't know how to git the country out of the scrape you've got it in, the people will tell you pretty quick, or I aint no hand at guessin. I have now done my duty. If the people don't do theirn it aint my fault. If they say my notions are right they 'll act on em ; if they say they are wrong, then things will go on as they now go, and I hope they won't git worse---but that I wont promise. If things come to the worst, 1 shall suffer as little as any on em, for I haint got no wife and children to support (and I am sorry for those who have, if things are to go as they now go,) I can cut my fodder pretty much any where.

But I love my country, every acre on't, and it goes agin my grain to see any part on't suffer. And I know all this suffering comes from party politics---this same party politics that has driv all our wisest and best men out of office ; and now to keep together wants to get hold of the big wagon and all the money in it.

My dander is up, and I best stop now---for the more I think on't, and the more I write about it, the more wrathy I git. So no more at present,

From your fellow citizen,

J. DOWNING, Major,
Downingville Militia, 2d Brigade.

MAJOR JACK DOWNING ENTERING THE CABINET WITH HIS AXE.

LETTER LXX.

The Major carries the axe, sent to him as a present from Carthage, N. Y. over his shoulder into the Cabinet while the members were in Council, the scampering that followed the sight of it, and the result— with a true picture of the scene.

To my old friend Mr. Dwight of the New York Daily Advertiser.

WASHINGTON, 10th January, 1834.

The pill I give the Cabinet, and the rest of the Government here on the 27th of last month, is jist beginnin to operate, and I dont think some on 'em will want any more fisik for a good spell to come. Some of our folks make plagy ugly faces at me, but I told 'em that's a sure sign they want fisik, and they'd feel better to rights. It was well I stop'd jist where I did in that Cabinet paper, for my dander was jist liftin; and if I had gone on ten minits longer, I'd hit some on 'em so hard they would'nt swell.

But that aint what I want to write you about now. I want to thank them folks up in Carthage, in York State for the ax they made for me, and which they sent to you to send to me. I have jist got it, and it has tickled me eny most to death. I never got such a present afore in my born days. I started right up chamber with it to the Gineral, and bolted strait into the Cabinet room with my ax on my shoulder—the Gineral was there with pretty much all our folks overhauling the Post Office accounts, and tryin to git them straite, which is a plagy tuf job; but no matter: in I smash'd but afore I could git out one word, I never see such a scamperin. I turned to head some on 'em, jist to tell em what I was arter, but it seemed the more I tried, the more they tried to streak it, and in less than one minit there warnt a livin criter left but I and the Gineral; and the Gineral some how got a notion in his

head, and would a gone too, if there warnt no pluck in
him.   He was standin up with his back agin the man-
til tree, and his hickory in his hand, and look'd for all
the world as tho' he was jist expecting a fight.
   Why, says I. Gineral, what on earth is all this scampering for?   Well, says he, I reckon you can tell better than I can ; and with that, he blink'd at me most
plagily; and says he, what is the news now?   Why,
says I, there aint nothin new but this ere ax, and
I brought it to show you; its a present to me, says I
from Starks & Co., away up in York State, on the
Black River.   The Gineral changed face in a minit,
and it was jist like the sun risin.   He step'd up to me
and took the ax, and walk'd to his chair, and sat down,
and throw'd his head back, and ha haw'd right out.   It
does me good, in these times to see the Gineral tickled
at any thing.   As soon as the Gineral could say any
thing,—says he Major call back Tany and Barry and
Amos, and haw, haw, haw, says the Gineral; and jist
then, I got the notion why they all scampered off so ;
and sot down right in front of the Gineral, and we haw
hawd'd I tell you, for more than half an hour.
   And so to rights, we got talkin agin, and the Gineral he wiped his eye, and blew his nose jist for all the
world as tho' he had been cryin; and says he, Major,
it aint strange they was a leetle afeard of you, for do
you know jist as you come in, some on 'em was sayin
about the plagy Post Office accounts.   If they did'nt
git em strait pretty soon, you would git at 'em and
chop em all up into mince meat; and jist then sure enuf
in you come, and then haw, haw, haw, says the Gineral agin.   Well, says he, Major, I'm glad that people
about are beginnin to look at you pretty much as I do.
I knew, says he, the time would come when they would
say I knew what was what when I got you to be with
me; and says he Major, let's look at this ax, and the
Gineral he rubb'd his specs; well says he, this is a
splitter aint it; why, says he, if a man only got lath-
ered he could shave himself without a barber, for

for this ax is as bright as a looking glass and sharp as a razor; and here is the maker's name too: " Starks & Co.' Carthage, New York" I do wonder now, says the Gineral, if that aint the same "Stark" who lick'd the British at Benington a spell ago?" "I aint certin," says I. "Well, nor I nother," says the Gineral, for do you know Major I have been in so many wars myself, that I some times mix em up, and I have now got so much to attend to here, that I am bother'd about names and places and times, most plagily. Now there is our little district attorney, our folks telled me when I appointed him a Bank Director that he was jist the kind of man we wanted "to ride Biddle" and upset him; and when they tell'd of " ridin " " upsettin, and mentioned his name, I got a notion in my head that I can't get out yet, that he may be the same man I've heard tell on, who took a ride once, and then wrote a long account on't in poetry. Well, says I, I'm not certain of that nother; but I've got a notion that the man you mean was John Gilpin. " That's the same man, aint it," says the Gineral. No, says I, I guess it aint, for he lived in London. " O, that makes no odds," says he Gineral; " for they used to call Philadelphia the Lond n of America." Well says I, then it must be the same, and if he's got on the squire to ride him, I guess it will turn out pretty much such another ride; for, says I, the squire is a pretty good horse for a tight pull; but I don't think he'd stand easy under a saddle; it aint the natur of that breed.

Well Major, says the Gineral, we must thank those folks for the ax any how, and as soon as the Senate pass, upon that message we sent em t'other day about other presents, you can have the ax. Very well, says I, Gineral, and if Congress dont pass upon something else, says I, so as to git things as leetle better in the money way, I'll want the ax, for we shall all come to choppin agin for a livin.

I want you to send a printed copy of that letter to the makers of that ax, and when you git all my letters to you printed in a book send em one of the books with my thank, for the ax.

Your friend,

J. DOWNING. Major.

Downingville Militia---2d brigade,

LETTER LXXI.

The Major and the President holds a general conversation on the state of the Nation, when the Major gives an explanation of the financial operations as now conducted, by means of hocus pocus, with cups and balls.

To my old friend Mr. Dwight, of the New York Daily Advertiser.

Washington, 25th Jan. 1834.

Ever since I and the Gineral settled the Post Office accounts, as I tell'd you in my last, by charging the amount that Major Barry is astern, to "Glory" and "Reform," the Gineral has been more easy about it than I am afeard other folks be, especially some of the opposition folks in Congress; they keep smellin round—and unless we can git up another nullification there will be trouble, not only about the Post Office, but some other branches of the Department.

Congress keeps hammering away yet about the deposits, and the Gineral was gist agoin to give up, when we got the news from Albany of the vote of the Legislatur there in favor of the Gineral in taking away the deposits from the United States Bank, and the vote of the New Jersey Legislatur, and strong news too that some other Legislaturs wo'd do the same. The Gineral was amazingly tickled, and says he, Major, I reckon your notion that the people wornt with us on that pint is a mistake, and now says the Gineral, I'll hang on and keep the deposits, and Biddle may whistie for 'em. "Well," says I, "Gineral we'll see, and as I said afore, if the people don't tell the Legislaturs another story, and Congress too, afore we are a month older, then," says I, "I know nothing on em. "Very well, Major," says the Gineral, "we'll see"—and jest then in come Amos and the Globe man, and some more of our folks, and lookin pretty streaked too, and I got a notion right off there was somethin stirrin—and os they began to tell the Gineral and Biddle was to work bribin all the people he could to sign petitions to Congress, asking to put back in the Bank all the deposits agin, and to recharter the Bank. "Why," says the Gineral, "aint that too bad,—Major we must give the Bank, says he, that Latin pill, there is nothin will stop em but that skiry factus" (or some sich a name the Gineral calls it.) Now, says I, Gineral, stop a bit, says I—there is one thing puzzles me considerable about this bribin business—I should like to know who they be who are takin bribes—it aint the nature of things, says I, for Squire Biddle to bribe the friends of the Bank, for that would be useless—then, says I, it must be that he is bribin the enemies of the Bank, and that's our party. Now, says I will you set by and hear folks say, that our party is such a scabby set of fellows as to take bribes—if you do, says I, I wont, and with that I riz up, but before I could round the corner of the table I and the Gineral was alone agin. I sat down and said nothin—I gritted my teeth a spell, but that didn't do much good—I took my knife and whittled the table. but that warnt much better, and the ony way to rights that put me in a good temper agin, was to whistle more than 40 verses of Yankee Doodle, for I didn't like to say a word to the Gineral whilst I was in a pashin. The Gineral was all the while walkin up and down the room—so as soon as I got through whistlin, says I Gineral, I guess we best say nothin more about bribin, says I; well, says he, Major, 1 reckon you are riget, for the notion never struck me afore that that kinder talk hits right upon the heads of our friends, for they are the only ones that needs bribin. Now, says

I, Gineral, jest lets you and I sit down and talk over this business, and I'll tell you, like a true friend, how the cat is goin to jump, and if it don't turn out as I tell you, I'll give you my ax, and throw in my regimentals in the bargain; and so the Gineral he sot down, and I went at it.

In the first place, says I, if I git in a pashin, you must keep cool—and if you git in a pashin I'll keep cool, but if we both git in a pashin, then there's no tellin. Well, says the Gineral, that's a good notion, Major, for that's jest the way the Ingins do, and they learn wisdom from natur; you never see an Ingin and his squaw git drunk together—when one gits drunk tother keeps sober, and so they take turn and turn about. Well says I, I never heard that afore, but I suppose tho' they git along better when they are both sober. O yes, says the Gineral, in war time that is best, but not in treaty time. Well, says I, that's matter, that aint exactly what I am arter, but I've got a notion out on't which I'll begin with. Some years ago the Yankees got drunk and got up a kinder nullification; there warnt much in it arter all, according to my old friend Dwight's book—but folks South thought there was, and so they kept sober; and last year the South got drunk, and then all North kept sober, and that frolic is ended. Now, says I, North and South and East and West are all sober, and all shaken hands, and they say *we* have all been takin a drop too much—there aint no nullification no where in particular, but its all nullification all about us, and all hands are formin a ring and closin in upon us here, pretty much like a wolf hunt—they all say we have taken the money that belongs to the people, and the people wont be content till we give it up—that's pretty much the *nub* of the business—and we shall have petitions and memorials from all quarters tumble in upon us, and if we don't mind them, they will be follow'd by hard nocks, jest like the story in the Spellin Book about the old man drivin the boys from the apple tree—he throw'd grass

S

first, and that doing no good, he tried stones, and that brought em down pritty quick.

The Gineral he began to git in a pashin—and says he Major I'm gittin mad. Very well says I Gineral I'll keep cool accordin to agreement: and with that the Gineral slatted round a spell with his hickory, and talked about New Orleans—and Siminoli—and the Grand tower—and I set whistling all the while—" why Major, says the Gineral, I'll never give up the deposites in the world"—" what" says I, " not if the people say we was wrong in takin em? Suppose the people say the laws are agin us, what then?"—" Well says the Gineral I've tell'd em that the Laws are only jest as I understand em and nothing else." Now says I, Gineral, suppose Clay, or Calhoun, or Webster, was in your office and said so—and you was in Congress, or was of the people and didn't agree with em—how then says I? O, says the Gineral, that's a very different thing; any one of them fellows would be dangerous to trust with any kind of power. Well says I my notion is, however, that the law don't mean to trust nobody—and as I am peskily afeard one or tother on'em will git in here arter we go to the Hermitage—I don't want to have any thing done now by us that they will do, and then tell us they ony do what we did. That's the only thing that puzzles me—for says I, Gineral, sass for the goose ought to be sass for the gander too.

Well, says the Gineral, there is something in that Major—but says he, I cant give up the Deposits any how; Amos says we must hold on to 'em, and all our folks say so too. Yes, says I. Gineral, its true enuff the hounds have got the stag down, and got a taste on him afore the hunters come up, and I suppose there will be leetle left but the horns and trotters: but, says I, it aint right, and the people will tell us so you may depend: and all I have to say is, if what we have done is to be the rule hereafter, I dont know but I should like to be President myself: for folks might make laws, and all I'd have to do would be to understand 'em according to my notion.

I dont see Major, says the Gineral, how it is you git
sich odd notions about public sentiment. I know I
cant be mistaken, for every letter I have time to read
tells me I am right; and I read the Globe from one eend
to tother every day, and that paper tells every thing,
and I see nothin there that tells me I am rong.----Well,
says I, Gineral you know you haint got time to read
more than one letter in a nundred that comes. That's
true enuf, says the Gineral, but then our folks do, and
they tell me every thing. Tell you every thing? says
I,---but no matter?---and so I whistled Yankee Doodle
a spell. "No, No, Major, says the Gineral, the opposition folks throw dust in your eyes, you cant see
things as clear as the rest of our folks about us." I jest
was goin to speak, but findin my dander was liftin, I
had to go to whistlin agin, and it took me nigh upon 15
minits to git right, and I expected evry minit, I would
have to git my ax and split hickory a spell in the bargain. Now, says I Gineral, you are the only man on
earth I'd look at a minit, and let him say so to me. I
got dust in my eyes, says I? I dont know what is goin
on in doors and out of doors? Why says I, how you
talk. Now says I, you jist sit still a minit and I'll
show you something says I worth lookin into---and I
went into a room where Mr. Van Buren and Amos and
some of our folks git together every once and a while, to
manage and talk over matters, and I've seen so much
of the games play'd there, and bein naturally curious
in most matters, I can play some on 'em nigh upon as
slick as Mr. Van Buren himself----but he is master hand
at it.---The game they had been playin most at latterly,
was about managin the public money among the new
Deposit Banks, and showin how to use the *"transfer
checks"* and *"contingent drafts"* so as to puzzle folks
in time of need. It was done with a parcel of cups
and balls, and little strips of paper—and did tickle me
amazingly; and for a spell puzzled me tu---and so I
thought I'd jist show the Gineral and see if it would'nt
tickle and puzzle him tu. And I thought I'd let the

Gineral see if there warn't a leetle dust in his eyes tu.
And so I brought in a whole arm full of this machinery.
And as soon as the Gineral saw me, says he Major
what on earth have you got there.---Why, says I, its a
trifle, and I'll tell you all about it to rights. And so I
placed the cups bottom up, all along in a row on the
table, and then I gin the Gineral a hand full of small
balls. Now says I, I'm goin to show you about as cute
a thing as you've seen in many a day---them cups we'll
call banks, and them balls is the money we took from
Squire Biddle's Bank, the next thing is to show you
how things are goin to work, now that we've got our
money from one pocket, where we always know'd where
to find it, and divided it round among twenty pockets,
where may-be you may, or may-be you may not find
nothin at all on't-- and here says I are some leetle
pieces of paper that I'm goin to make use on to throw
dust with---now says I Gineral, look sharp or you're
gone hook and line says I. Its a plagy cunnin game,
and I don't know sartin that I can play it as well as
Mr. Van Buren and Amos and some more of them are
folks, and 'specially the Treasury folks, for they have
been at it now off and on ever sense I've been here---
and Mr. Van Buren tell'd em unless they could play
at *this game* well, there was no use in takin away the
deposits. Now says I Gineral I'll begin---you are sartin says I there is a ball under every cup.---O yes says
the Gineral, for I jest put em there, and then begun
sliden the cups by each other, and mixin on em, and
kept talkin about Glory and Reform---and the 8th 'o
Jinnewerry, and the Proclamation, and Veto, and
Nul lification, and some folks ben like Old Romans
born to Command! and others to obey, and so on, and
jest as the Gineral took his eye off the cups and look'd
at me, an was goin to say somthin, I slap'd som cups
together and call'd out hocuspocus, allicumpain, presto!
e pluritus unum, sine qua non, skiry factions, says I---
there says I Gineral that's the eend on't. Well says
the Gineral I dont see much in that Major---didn't you.

says I? then so much the better for the game. I suppose then says I you think the balls are under the cups, and jest as you put them. To be sure I do, says the Gineral, I suspected what you was ater Major, and I kept my eye on the cups; and no balls ever get from under 'em without me seein 'em I'd stake my life on't says the Gineral; and whats more I'll stake the fastest horse in my stable, that every one of the cups has got a ball under 'em. Well says I, Gineral, it wouldn't be fare bettin, and so do you go to work and look. And the Gineral he lifted up the cup, and there warn't nothin under it but a piece of paper. The Gineral, he was stump'd, he look'd at me and gin his face a twist, and then he look'd in the cup and shook it. Well. says he Major, that is plagy odd, what has become of that ball? Well, says I, I guess the paper will tell you; and the Gineral took up that, and rub'd his specks and read, "Transfer draft No. 101." Well then I suppose, says the Gineral, its all right---(for he had jist begun to take the notion of the game) and insted of one ball in the next cup there is two balls."---"I'm not sartin, says I, and you better look. And so the Gineral lifted the next cup---and there warnt no balls there nother--- ony another piece of paper. The Gineral look'd a spell at me, and opened his mouth, and then he scratched his head, and took off his specks, and rub'd them agin, and then he read the paper. On one side was, "Contingent check $500,000—and on tother side was written "Marquess of Carmarthen," $250,000-6 per ct.— "Post office loans," and all kiver'd up with figures so you could not see a bit of "White" on the paper---the Gineral, he blink'd at it a spell; and says he, Major, what does this mean; well, says I, Gineral, I dont exactly know myself but I suppose its all right, for I see here on one corner "Amos Kindle"---"O very well, says the Gineral, if that paper has past under the eye of 'honest Amos'---my life on't its all right. But, Major, where is the ball I put under that cup, says the Gineral---aint it under one of these cups? Not as I

knows on, says I---and with that the Gineral he turned
to agin, liftin the cups and shakin on 'em and lookin
into 'em, and there warnt under any one on 'em ; only
---ony pieces of paper all full of figures, and some on
'em marked *"Transfer Checks,"* and *"Contingent
Drafts,"* and *"Treasury Warrants,"*---the Gineral hussled em about to see if he could find any of them balls
among em---and examined all the cups agin, and he
looked under the tables---so to rights, says he, Major,
I'm stump'd---I nock under---I'm clean beat, says the
Gineral; and now, says he, where are the balls---and
with that I put my hand in my pocket, and took em out
---well, says the Gineral, that beats all the rest.   Now,
says the Gineral, what game is this, aint this nickremancy? Well says I, Gineral, my notion is its pretty
nigh that, but Mr. Van Buren says there aint a bit of
nickremancy in it---it's ony financery, but I suppose it's
a leetle of both on em. ---Well, says the Gineral, its a
plagy cunnin game, Major, aint it? O, says I, its nothin
as I play it here---you should see Van Buren at one eend
of a table, and honest Amos at tother, and some of the
folks from York State with the "Safety Funds cups" too,
strung around the table, and all on em understandin
the game nigh upon as well as Mr. Van Buren, and then
they bring in the "party cups" too---and such a movin
and hocuspocus work, I never see afore in my born days
---in lookin sometimes I would'nt bet I had a head on
my shoulders---it beats all natur says I.

Now Major, says the gineral, suppose you try it agin,
and so as I got my hand in, I played it over 2 or 3 times a
leetle better, and the gineral couldn't see the trick no
way---for when I'd find him watchin plagy close, I'd
spread the cups as far as I could reach, and talked about
" Glory" like all rath, and tell about the people's beginnin to think that some folks was outwittin the gineral,
and that congress wouldn't go home afore they git all the
public counts sifted, and the people's money back agin
under their control, and the gineral couldn't no way keep
his eye on all the cups at once, I'd *hocus pocus* agin. The

gineral couldn't see into it, and he rub'd his specks more than twenty times, but that didn't get the dust out of his eyes, and then I turn'd to and explain'd all I know'd about it to the gineral, and he tried it, and after a good many slips---pretty much as Major Barry did when he tried it---he got along pretty well considerin. Now, Major, says the gineral, suppose we try it with one cup, and put all the balls under it, and see how the game works that way. I think says the gineral, if you can outwit me then, I may as well quit. Well, says I, gineral that was jest my notion too; and I tell'd our folks, and offer'd to bet any on 'em they couldn't git a piece of paper in the place on't, without my seein it if they ony us'd one cup, and not one on 'em would take me up---and I've tried it, but it won't work with one cup---you must have a good string on 'em. Some of our folks said they could fix a cup so as to play the game with it---but they couldnt with a plain single cup---and seein that I stump'd 'em about the single cup, they are at work now in all parts of the country inventin a cup with springs, and screws, and slides, and holes inside on't. Well major, says the gineral, I don't like to have dust throw'd in my eyes, and I never did like this kind of *hocus pocus* work, I never understand it ; and I don't like this kind of *nickermancy*, or *financy*---and it aint to my *fancy* at any rate, Major, and it shan't be, that I'm determin'd upon; and jest then in come a hull raft of our folks from Congress, to tell the Gineral what was goin on there; and as I had this letter to write to you I went into the next room, and whilst I was writin it, I'd hear the Gineral once in a while stormin away about that plagy game of " *financy*" and " *nick-remancy*" " There won't be a dollar left," says the Gineral, " to pay the old sogers their pensions, if we don't put a stop to this game," and then they all got to blusterin, " and *we* must," and " we musn'nt do this and that." Oho, thinks I, when folks talk of *we* its time for me to take a hand; and jist as I was goin to to start, I heard the Gineral roar out for me, and not knowing what was comin I jist grab'd my ax, and was alongside of him in a flash; and would you think it? there was more than fifty fellows of our folks, and some on 'em from Congress too, all standing round in a ring; brow beating the Gineral, and tellin him not to do this, and not to do that, and by no means not to break their cups; for, it seems. the Gineral had jist threatened to smash 'em; and sure enuf, as soon as he saw me he let drive at 'em with his hickory, and he sent the cups and balls into more than a thousand bits. "Stand by Major" says the Gineral; never you fear me Gineral. says I; but afore I had time to spit in my hands, the Gineral finished the war; there warn a critter left. And ever sense, the Gineral has been blowin off steam ; and he haint said a word to me about havin dust in my eyes, and I begin to think the Gineral finds he has had as much in his'n as most folks. and so that's all for the present; only I'll jist tell you its no use for any one to attempt now to deceive the Gineral with new plans, and a new bank; we'll have the one we've got made a little bigger, pritty much arter Mr. Webster's fashion. and that meets my notion, because the country is bigger than it was 20 years ago; and there musn't be no nickremancy about it. The Gineral says there must be ony a plain cup, and balls in it; then there will be no hocus pocus without seein the trick out. So no more at present. From your friend,

J. DOWNING, Major,
Downingville Militia, 2d Brigade.

END.